Art to Wear
with
Asian Flair

By Stephanie Masae Kimura

Published by
Krause Publications
700 E. State St., Iola, WI
54990-0001

Please call or write for our free catalog of publications. Our toll-free number to place an order or obtain a free catalog is 800-258-0929 or please use our regular business telephone 715-445-2214.

All photography by Abbey of London or Stephanie Masae Kimura, unless otherwise noted.
On the cover, Kumiko Sodeyama and Beate Wilson are photographed by Abbey of London.

Library of Congress Catalog Number: 2001090487

ISBN: 0-87349-227-7

Acknowledgment

*t*his book is dedicated to my mother Edith, my mentors Linda Kardos M.D., Susan Braunstein Ph.D., Evelyn McMartin, and Susan Zaccheo; and Jean Jacobs and Gayle Boshek who encouraged me to teach.

I would like to thank my generous suppliers: Bernina® of America, Fairfield Processing, TWE Beads, Sulky® of America, Superior Threads, Trans Pacific Fabrics, and Zenga for Asian textiles. I am also grateful for the art-to-wear venues created by the Fairfield Fashion Show, Quilts Inc., and Peter and David Mancuso.

But my deepest appreciation goes to my editor, Jodi Rintelman, for turning mayhem into magic.

Table of Contents

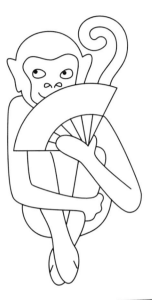

Chapter 5: Motif Templates

Introduction

Hawaii is a great place to grow up. My eyes feasted on every color of the spectrum. The fragrances took me off to places unknown. The sounds danced and lured me to smile. The cultures mingled and quickly offered their blessings.

Hawaiian, Samoan, Japanese, Chinese, Filipino, Portuguese, Korean, and Thai (just to name a few) festivals allowed me to become familiar with art, history, food, and music of all cultures. Lores of dragons, samurai, and the volcano goddess filled my life. Sometimes it was difficult to tell where tradition from one culture left off and another began. For instance, the Chinese New Year is still celebrated by everyone with as much significance as the traditional New Year.

A common thread with all of the cultures was the reverence of nature. Lives depended on the seasons, wind, rain, and sun. The color of the crops gave hint of the abundance to come. Color and everyday items held symbolic meaning. For example, the strength and endurance of bamboo has made it a symbol of longevity, honesty, and purity.

All of the motifs used in this book are still a part of everyday life in Hawaii. They can be found in architecture, a bank letterhead, a restaurant entrance, and on the uniform of a city employee. Creating art to wear with a little bit of history and a little bit of today results in a timeless garment ready to tell a story.

Art to wear became a part of my life at the age of thirteen. During the summers, I attended Mrs. Azama's sewing school in Pearl City on the island of Oahu. My friends and I planned what to make to wear for the coming school year. We spent weeks measuring, cutting, sewing, ripping out seams, more sewing, and always laughing. When we learned how to draft patterns, there was no stopping our creative minds. We made muumuus for Aloha Friday. We made Hapi coats for the Obon Festival, and we made cool, comfortable clothing suitable for a tropical climate.

This was the seed that grew into plans for my own business creating custom clothing. Although I originally designed and created everything from wedding gowns to beaded country western outfits, I was always drawn to clothing that reflected the multi-cultural images of Hawaii. To celebrate the year 2000, year of the Dragon, I designed *The Heart of a Golden Dragon* kimono ensemble for the Fairfield Fashion Show. The dragon on the back of the kimono was a blaze of sequins and beads and symbolized power, magnificence, and divinity while representing the richness of the Asian arts of my native Hawaii.

While collecting Asian fabrics, I created my own hand-dyed fabrics and found myself with a grouping of rich, earthy, and fiery fabrics reminiscent of volcanoes. I entered Linda McGehee's Fiber Art Challenge and won the Viewer's Choice award with an oversized handbag. It was made of richly textured silks embellished with metallic threads and appropriately called *Tropical Evolution*.

My first foray into the Sulky Challenge was with a vest inspired by the tropical seas of Southeast Asia. The vest made use of hand-dyed silks with vibrant turquoise, emerald green, and sapphire blue. Occasionally, there was a rippling of dimensional threads to emulate the wiggling sea life found deep under the sea. All of this was enhanced with the most brilliant metallic threads in a myriad of colors. This entry was named *Deep Sea Sonata* and won an Honorable Mention in the top ten.

All of these experiences allowed me to explore the culture of my heritage and express the past with the finest materials. What a great job this is to create beautiful garments and share them with others. I hope you are able to use this book to inspire you to create your own style with Asian flair.

The Morikami Museum and Japanese Gardens, Delray, Florida. Photo credit: Michiko Kurisu. This is a home away from home for me.

Overview of the Art

*a*sian art is as old as recorded history, as ancient as female wisdom, and as profound as the primal forces that urge women to seek beauty in their everyday lives. Although Asian flair is seen in some of the latest designs in haute couture, the timeless beauty and power of ancient cultures transcends trends. These designs are stylish, but beyond mere style. They are exotic, enigmatic, powerful, glamorous, and serene. When you create your own custom designed art to wear with an Asian flair, you connect with an ancient, honorable, and noble tradition of women bringing meaning and beauty into their lives and into the lives of the people around them.

To create your Asian flair, you will use sewing and quilting techniques, surface design, and embellishment. You can copy these designs, or you can use them to inspire your own creations. You are limited only by your imagination. Art to wear has no limits.

Free-motion and the appliqué stitch are the sewing and quilting techniques we will focus on. These two simple methods are versatile and allow you to create texture, dimension, and detail. Special threads and fabrics will inspire and help to create one-of-a-kind garments. Surface design with the aid of paints, inks, and fabric pens (that are heat set) will give you immediate artistic results. Rubber stamps and stencils aid in design control. The line drawings of motifs can be cut out of fabric, used for appliqué or free-motion quilting, or made into stencils and rubber stamps. Feel free to substitute any method.

Art-to-wear projects will guide you to make use of all the information available to you. The garment construction instructions are kept to a minimum, since the pattern that you choose (or create) will have its own specific instructions. The projects will have a list of supplies, fabric suggestions, and offer motif selections.

The selection of motifs was taken from vintage Asian textiles, most often from Japanese kimono and obi. The juxtaposition of images in Asian textiles tends to differ from fabric typically found in the United States. In this country, we tend to have prints that are arranged with some order of size, color, and direction. We tend to use conventional perspective and realism. Repeat of pattern is taken into account for the width and length of our fabric.

Because the kimono only came in one shape, without very much variation for size, all the fabric came in approximately 14" widths. The repeat of design or placement of asymmetrical design was purposefully done to accommodate the making of a kimono.

In kimono, asymmetrical designs send our eyes flowing from one "vignette" to the next. Because of Asia's own "perspective style," pine trees seem to float with cranes, fans are found surrounded by water, and flowers may be in profusion everywhere. Auspicious symbolic meaning creates designs where plum, bamboo, and pine are clustered and seem to grow together to convey longevity, hope, happiness, and good luck.

It will take a bit of planning to decide on the size and number of motifs to use on the limited area available on a jacket or vest. I separated the "vignettes" to allow the enjoyment of the shape and color of each motif in relation to the next. The sewing techniques were taken into consideration when creating the size of the details.

The color combinations used on Asian textiles can sometimes be categorized by season, age of the wearer, and occasion for the textile. All colors are used all the time but are changed by shade, tint, intensity, and combination to suit the category. Feel free to use the colors that appeal to you, and do not feel limited by realism or tradition.

The shapes of the garments created in the guided projects are contemporary and comfortable. The jackets and vests, adorned with these treasured motifs and fabrics, will prove to be timeless. These garments are meant to be worn and enjoyed. This is truly the fusion of American style with Asian flair.

Beginning Projects with Basic Supplies

there are many methods for applying the motifs and designs to your wearable art. These same techniques have been used on textiles for centuries. These products are new and improved, but the results are basically the same. With the use of today's dyes, inks, stamps, and stencils, the art of the past can be reproduced with very little time and effort, leaving more time to enjoy art to wear.

The ink and fabric pens dry quickly to allow for immediate use. The dyes allow more time, movement, and blending of color to encourage creative surface design techniques. Rubber stamps and stencils will aid in design control and the accurate and swift repetition of motifs. The erasable ink used in combination with the rubber stamps and stencils will offer temporary guides.

The inks, dyes, and resists are water based and are selected for their ease of use, while offering quality results. The resist can be used with both inks and dyes, and it shares the same techniques. Try both products, and use them for projects that suit your designs.

Inks

Inks are different from dyes. When painted onto fabric, they render an opaque quality and slightly change the feel of the fabric. Inks are available in many colors. They have wonderfully descriptive names—ash rose, wisteria, autumn leaf, tangerine, and lemon yellow to name a few. The concentrated inks can be mixed with each other to create even more colors, or they can be mixed with water to create a lighter color or a pastel.

The inks tend to flow a little more slowly and will flow shorter distances than dyes. Once they start to dry, the inks will not move at all. The inks are then set permanently. (They should be pressed with an iron and pressing cloth just to be safe. Use a setting on your iron suitable for the fabric.) All of this is an advantage when more control over the application is needed and the results are needed immediately.

You will need:

* ❋ Inks, dyes, and fabric pens
* ❋ Resists
* ❋ Brushes and Fantastix
* ❋ Fabrics
* ❋ Frames and hoops
* ❋ Rubber stamps and foam brushes
* ❋ Stencils and a cutter

Tsukineko All-Purpose Inks are available in many colors and can be mixed to create even more colors.

Dyes

The dyes used in these projects are selected because of their vibrant, translucent colors and their versatility. The dyes are easily blended into a myriad of colors. They add another dimension to the garment by allowing the sheen of the fabric to enhance the color. The dyes are very concentrated and can be mixed with water to create a lighter color or pastel. They flow freely and quickly on smooth fabric.

When the dyes are dried, they can be layered with more dye (to create another color), sprayed with water (to rejuvenate the dyes and create more movement), and manipulated with alcohol (to diffuse the dye). All of which create interesting textures. The dyes are not permanent, until they have been set with a liquid fixative for five minutes.

Even after the dyes have been set with a fixative, more dye can be added. Then the fabric can be placed in the fixative again. This liquid fixative was created to be used with these dyes. The fixative is mixed with water according to the directions. A shallow plastic pan can be used to set a lot of yardage. The fixative can also be painted onto the silk. This method is ideal for small areas of dyed fabric.

Dyes are great for creating a lot of yardage. Especially if the fabric is scrunched up damp or dry and placed on a plastic sheet on the floor. Spray, spill, or paint your favorite colors (or colors leftover from projects). Let them slowly blend together by covering them with more plastic.

When the white of the fabric is gone and the fabric is still damp, sprinkle it with small amounts of salt. Use any texture, from small grains of table salt to large granules of sea salt. The salt will attract the dye, creating wonderful striations and mixtures of color.

Fabrics

The choice of fabrics will have an effect on the process of applying dyes and inks. Inks work well on both silks and cottons, while these dyes are made to be used on silks. A finer, smoother weave will allow the inks and dyes to travel quickly and evenly. A few examples of this are Crepe de Chine silk, china silk, and silk charmeuse. The dyes and inks spread faster when the fabric is stretched taut with a frame or hoop. If the fabric is not stretched but placed over a few layers of paper towel, the painted area will stay somewhat confined but still move slowly. The excess dye or ink will escape to the paper towel. For best results, use untreated natural fabrics.

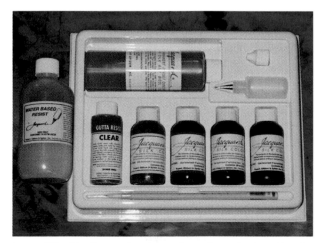

Jacquard Dye Kit: Resist and applicator, dyes, silk paintbrush, and liquid fixative.

Resist

The use of a resist will allow you greater freedom in designing your images. A resist does just that; it resists the dyes and inks. Resists are available in clear, black, gold, and other colors. If clear is used, it will retain the original color of your fabric. If black is used, it will retain that black line.

The image is traced onto the silk, using erasable ink. Then the silk must be stretched taut. Round hoops, square frames, and specially constructed fabric-stretcher frames can be purchased or made.

The resist is applied over the erasable-ink lines, which will disappear. Your designs should be planned with simple and unbroken lines. This will contain the ink or keep it out.

Keep the silk evenly flat. Hold the bottle of resist vertically, allowing the tip to press lightly against the fabric. Squeeze the bottle gently, while following the erasable guidelines. The amount of resist released, coordinated with how quickly your hand moves, will determine how thin or thick these lines will be. The size of the applicator tip and the consistency of the resist will also affect your lines. (The applicator tip comes in fine, medium, and large. Water-based resist can be thinned with water.)

When the resist is dry, check it from the reverse side for broken lines. For best results, let the resist dry before adding the inks and dyes.

The image is traced onto silk, in this case with a handmade stencil.

The silk is stretched taut. Gold resist is applied in a continuous stroke with unbroken lines.

Finish one area before painting another.

Fill in with a solid color, or use light strokes with dye or ink diluted with water for a lighter color and watercolor effects.

There are no broken lines for the dye or ink to seep out.

Fabric pens

Fabric pens are versatile. They can be used alone (on a variety of fabrics) or in combination with other products.

The fabric pen and the use of a light table will allow you to trace any image onto almost any fabric. The fabric pens come in a variety of colors. They also have tips that create a brush-like effect, a bullet tip that produces wide lines, and a fine tip for details.

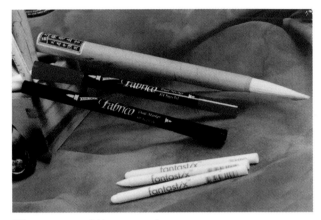

Fabric pens are available in many colors.

Sometimes the resist line is not fine enough and can be used in combination with fabric pens. Quick and sweeping lines with a light touch on the fabric can be used to trace all the lines on a selected motif. The harder you press on the fabric, the more ink the pen will release. If too much ink is released, the lines will bleed. Fabric pens and resist can be used with the Geisha's face, used in the *Maiko Celebration Vest*, page 65.

Brushes

Almost any brush can be used with different methods of application to create a multitude of effects with the inks and dyes. Just a few are mentioned here.

A short-haired, small, firm brush is handy as an all-purpose brush. This brush can be used to apply resist as well as inks and dyes. This brush can also be used to apply different mediums onto the rubber stamps instead of using a stamp pad.

The silk painting brushes are excellent and can be used with both the inks and dyes. The fine point allows for the control of dispersing a very small amount of ink and dye into tiny corners, yet when pressed onto the fabric, this brush can unload and quickly fill an area with color.

When applying ink or dye, hold the silk painting brush upright, and just touch the fabric to apply color. Be careful with painterly brush strokes, as they will push the dyes, which travel quickly and jump the resist lines.

When using inks, be careful not to let the brush dry. Place the brush in water, and rinse it as soon as possible. When using dyes, the dried dye on the brush can be washed out. In both cases, it is best to wash the brush with a mild soap and rinse it thoroughly, so the next color used will not be affected.

Fantastix™

The Fantastix coloring tools are uninked, disposable or reusable coloring applicators. They are available with a pointed brush tip or a rounded bullet tip. Fantastix are made of a resilient material that holds inks and dyes and works like a cross between a brush and a felt tipped pen.

The fantastix coloring tool is available with a pointed brush tip for detail and a rounded bullet tip for wide sweeps of color.

Fantastix can apply color as well as blend. Dip the tool in ink, and apply directly to the fabric for full-strength, accurate color. Then quickly dip the tool in water, and apply it to the ink to create a watercolor effect.

Keep a Fantastix tool handy for leaks in broken lines of resist. Use it to blot up unwanted color, and use it wet to disperse and push back small amounts of ink or dye.

Rubber stamps

Rubber stamps are offered in many designs and sizes. Rubber stamps created for fabric use larger images with bolder lines. They are generally kept to a manageable size. The best way to decide what to use is to try the stamp on various types of fabrics, using thickened inks and dyes, stamp pads, and resist. The designs should result in a clear, acceptable image.

Be sure to press your fabric and keep it as smooth as possible before stamping. Rubber stamps can be held with the image facing upright and the stamp pad held in your other hand. Lightly tap the image with the inked stamp pad. This allows you to get the color evenly on the image and not all over the recessed area of the stamp. Rubber stamps can also be used to apply erasable ink as guidelines for sewing techniques.

If a special motif cannot be found, a custom stamp can be ordered. Find a local rubber stamp company, and supply them with camera-ready art. Have the motif drawn in the actual size with clear, bold lines. Get an estimate. They charge by the square inch. Craft stores also sell rubber tiles and carving instruments to create your own stamps. Choose a motif from the examples in chapter 5, or design your own.

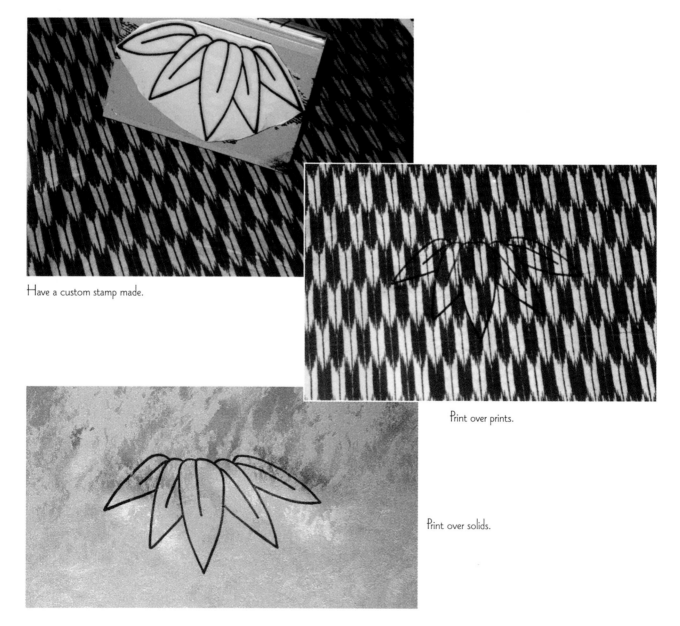

Have a custom stamp made.

Print over prints.

Print over solids.

For a small, overall repeat of motifs, stamp the motifs and draw connecting lines to follow. Do this while the fabric is flat and pressed. Then layer the fabric over batting and muslin to quilt with the free-motion technique. Larger patterns with simple lines can be used with the satin stitch technique.

The erasable-ink stamp pad combined with a stamp creates a guideline.

The image from the stamp is placed on the fabric in a random manner.

Then lines are drawn from motif to motif to trace with free-motion.

Stencils

Stencils used for fabric can offer the same detail that rubber stamps can produce, and they are not limited in size. Stencils are readily available and offer many designs, including borders. They work on all fabrics and are limited only by the medium used. A thickener can be added to dyes and inks to prevent them from bleeding when they are applied with a stencil. The thickener is a clear medium. When it is added, the color will be true. The thickener will not dilute the ink or dye. It has the same consistency as the resist, which allows for more control during application. It is available for purchase with the dyes and resist.

Preparing the ink

1. Add a thickener to the inks, and mix thoroughly, following the directions provided with the product.

2. Lightly apply the thickened inks with a foam brush or the Fantastix coloring tool.

3. After setting the thickened inks with heat, wash thoroughly with cold water. The thickener will wash out, leaving the original ink color.

Creating your own stencils

1. Use sheets of plastic specifically made for stencils to create strong and sturdy stencils. The sheets can be found in craft stores, in the same area where stencils are found. They are also available in some quilting and sewing shops, as they are also used to create templates for appliqués.

2. Use a stencil cutter that uses heat to melt away lines. (This tool gets very hot, and extra care is needed when working with it.) These stencil cutters are available in craft stores.

3. Select a motif that is simple, and trace it onto paper.

4. Make markings where the lines will be cut away and spaces for areas that will stay intact.

5. Place the plastic sheet over the drawing, and trace the drawing onto the plastic with a permanent marker. Remove the drawing, and tape the plastic sheet to a piece of glass to protect the area from harm by the heat of the cutter.

The plastic sheet is placed over the drawing and traced with a permanent marker.

6. Work on a very sturdy table. Practice using the cutter to make straight and curved lines. Hold the cutter as indicated on the instructions. There is a thickly padded rubber area to hold for protection from the intense heat.

Hold the cutter upright.

7. Hold the cutter upright, like a pen, allowing the full rounded tip to contact the plastic.

8. Start at the beginning of a line, moving slowly and deliberately, keeping the cutter moving at a consistent speed.

Cut along the lines, leaving some areas uncut.

9. When you reach the end of the line, carefully lift up the cutter. If it creates a thread of plastic, use a very thick wadding of paper towels to catch it. Also use paper towels to wipe any excess plastic stuck to the tip. (Remember, the tip is very hot and can quickly heat through many layers of paper towels.)

10. When the stencil is complete, unplug the cutter and place it on a safe surface to cool off. Use a razor or an X-Acto® knife to clear away any pieces of plastic remaining in the channels.

Clear away any excess plastic.

Stabilizer as a stencil

1. To transfer a design using lightweight stabilizer, place the stabilizer over the design, and trace it with a pencil. You may have to test several stabilizers to find one sheer, yet stable enough. Lightweight tear-away stabilizers work well.

2. Place the stabilizer with the design onto the fabric, where the design is to be transferred. Trace the design with a permanent ink marker or erasable ink. The inks will seep through the web-like stabilizer material and leave a guideline.

3. Carefully lift the stabilizer off the design, let the fabric dry, and use the stabilizer as a stencil again.

Trace over lines through the stabilizer.

This produces a faint line to follow.

Practicing with basic supplies

Cherry blossom blouse

Art to wear with Asian flair can be a quick and simple process. Adding motifs to ready-made garments creates an instant one-of-a-kind style. Start your art-to-wear wardrobe with a simple blouse.

When selecting a blouse, take into consideration the color, the motifs to be used, and the placement of the motifs. You may have something specific in mind, such as matching a vest or slacks.

Sometimes you can find inspiration from a work of art. The idea for using two shades of gold for the cherry blossom motifs came from the lining of a man's haori (shorter kimono worn as a jacket over the long kimono). These two shades also complemented the brushed gold closures down the center front of the blouse.

The purchased blouse before embellishment.

Left. The cherry blossoms and colors found on the haori displayed inside out were the inspiration.

Below. Close up of the lining.

Supplies

* Blouse
* Selection of fabrics: Two shades of gold dupioni silk
* Motifs: Cherry blossoms (see chapter 5)
* Thread: Gold metallic
* Lightweight batting
* Soft 'n Sheer™
* Tear-away stabilizer
* Spray adhesive

1. The cherry blossom motif is used in this project. Create a template, a stencil made of tear-away stabilizer, or make your own stencil.

2. Four flowers seemed right for this blouse. Add more or use less, depending on the size and style of your blouse.

Use a template or tear-away stabilizer...

...or create your own plactic stencil to transfer lines.

3. Trace and cut the cherry blossoms. Cut an equal number from both shades of gold dupioni silk.

4. Mark the placement of the flowers with a chalk pencil. Two dark gold flowers with one light gold flower in between are placed on the left side of the blouse. One light gold flower is placed on the lower right.

5. Lightly spray adhesive on the backs of the flowers. Place the flowers within the chalk markings, and lightly hand-press them into the blouse fabric. Place a few pins through each flower to help keep them in place.

6. Cut four squares of lightweight batting, Soft 'n Sheer, and tear-away stabilizer. Layer them in that order. Place each set underneath the blouse (one set behind each flower).

7. Pin through the dupioni silk, blouse fabric, and three layers underneath. Hand baste if your blouse fabric is delicate, or if it's difficult to keep all of the layers smooth.

8. To keep with a somewhat monochromatic scheme, gold metallic thread is selected. The shiny gold fabric and buttons are enough without adding another color.

9. Use a preliminary straight stitch, starting at the inside corner of a petal, and stitch around each flower. Stay close to the edge, and make sure not to twist or stretch the flower. Continue around the perimeter of the flower, returning to the initial inside corner. Repeat the process for all of the flowers. This stitch will be covered with the satin stitching.

10. Use a medium width satin stitch, starting at the inside corner of a petal. Make sure the width of the stitch covers the preliminary straight stitch as well as the edge of the flowers. Treat the tips of the petals as corners. When creating a corner, sew to the tip. For a left turn, swing your needle to the right side, and place your needle in the down position. Pivot the fabric. Start forward, going over the previous stitching. For a right turn, swing the needle to the left side, and place your needle in the down position. Pivot the fabric. Start forward, going over the previous stitching. Continue down the other side of the petal, and repeat until you return to the initial inside corner of the first petal. Repeat the process for all of the flowers.

11. With all the flowers completed, remove the tear-away stabilizer. Trim away excess Soft 'n Sheer and batting. Trim close to the stitching.

12. Use the basic backstitch found in the Embellishment section (page 45) to add a few beads in the center of the flower.

Close up of the cherry blossoms with the satin stitching and pearl bead embellishment.

Chapter 2

The Creative Process

Selecting a pattern

When selecting a pattern, consider the suitability of the pattern to the shape of your body, whether the designs will fit, and the expertise required. The construction of the clothing in this book is basic and uncomplicated, allowing more time for the enjoyment of creative design. This ensures a good fit and a fabulous work of art. I have used patterns that I have designed. My patterns can be found on my website (www.kimurapatterns.com) and at stores listed in the resource section of this book. Wonderful Asian-inspired patterns are also available by other independent pattern designers such as: Paw Prints Pattern Company, Pavelka Design, Park Bench Patterns, June Colburn Designs II, Sewing Workshop, and Diane Ericson's Revisions. More information about these designers can be found in the resource section of this book.

Many of the jackets that I design have modified dolman sleeves. Dolman sleeves are attached to the body of the pattern, making for an easy, one-piece front and one-piece back. This also allows you to sew the shoulder/sleeve seam and continue with a design down the arm. Most alterations are done in the side seams, either extending or reducing the fabric. Alterations can also be done at the center back seam or at the center front. Keep a current and accurate list of your measurements. Check your measurements with that of the pattern, always allowing for ease.

If your garment will include batting, you may have to allow for even more ease. Also take into consideration the use of shoulder pads. Create a version of the garment with muslin. Make changes to the length of the garment and sleeves, then transfer the changes to the pattern. Once this is done, your pattern can be used over and over again without hesitation.

The vests that I design are basic in shape and don't have darts. This is done intentionally to allow as much space as possible for the artwork. A vest is usually such a small garment, and there are so many ideas for so little space.

If you already have a pattern in mind, look at all the details such as darts, princess seam lines, and pockets. Pockets can be used creatively or hidden in a side seam. If there are set-in sleeves, see if you can work your designs around them. Most of all, make sure you will be comfortable.

Selecting fabric

This is the most exciting part of a project. You will find that adding fabric with Asian design to your collection will result in a wonderful fusion of art and fashion.

Vintage fabrics

Chinese silks are beautiful and can be found with dragons, flowers, and a multitude of motifs woven into the cloth. They range from subtle to vibrant and from light silks to heavy brocades. Vintage Chinese silk garments are exquisite and rare, and sometimes they can be found embellished with lustrous silken chords and embroidery.

Until recently, Indian saris were extremely expensive and rare. They are available now at quilt shows everywhere. The sari is basically a rec-

Vintage kimono fabric from a little girl's kimono, with traditional colors of purples, greens, and oranges.

tangle of fabric worn simply and traditionally over a specific base garment. This is a great advantage because the pieces are large, flat, and ready to cut. Each piece is excitingly different from the next. There are gossamer, sheer fabrics with gold threads woven along the selvage, and there are heavier fabrics with mirrors and beads added.

The Japanese kimono is made in a basic shape, size, and length. It is held together with a stiff sash called the obi. Over the decades, the Japanese have used a variety and combination of fibers. They also use different methods of applying dyes, weaving, and adding texture. Vintage kimono are easier to find and reasonably priced at this time. As more and more vintage kimono are taken from Japan, they will become difficult to acquire and the prices are sure to go up.

The kimono is lined with silk, which is sometimes edged with dye in a gradation of color. This added fabric gives the designer a lot to work with. When taken apart, the fabrics are narrow in width, approximately fourteen inches. The hand-sewn threads at the seams are old

and fragile. It is best to remove them, and then sew them back together with your sewing machine to create a larger cloth if needed.

The kimono can inspire you with motifs, color, and texture. Motifs can be taken from the fabric to continue the design concept to another part of the garment. The color combinations found in kimono can inspire you to use them with contemporary fabrics. The textures can vary due to the raised fibers in the weave as well as the intricate shibori (tie-dying) used to add color and create motifs. (The fiber content is unknown in kimono, but the threads can be burned to identify silk, wool, cotton, and polyester. Many times the fibers were combined.)

The obi is usually made of a heavier silk with the design in the weave. This results in a mass of threads on the reverse side.

When using the obi fabric, try to use it in combination with fabrics of similar weight. Some obi are made of lightweight fabric and just backed with a heavyweight material, which can be removed.

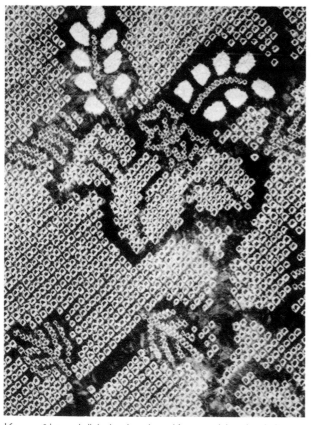

Kimono fabric embellished with traditional Japanese shibori (tie-dye), which creates a raised texture.

Kimono fabric with motifs and color combinations to inspire you.

When working with vintage textiles, dry-clean the fabric before using it if there is concern about the old stains. Sometimes even with dry-cleaning, the vintage fabric may disintegrate. This rarely happens, but it will save you the frustration of a ruined garment. Sometimes the fabric is so breathtaking that I use it in a wall hanging, which never needs to be laundered.

A fairly new obi with just these two designs.

Small designs found on a very old obi.

These motifs are found on a young boy's vintage kimono, with an interesting use of gold embroidery. The motifs include playful, chubby children and a Fu dog.

This is from an obi made with a sheer, summer weave. Paper is placed behind the motif to reveal the beautifully woven ship.

Cotton, rayon, and polyester fabric

Contemporary cotton, rayon, and polyester fabrics with Asian motifs can be found easily and in an array of colors. Many of these fabrics come in coordinated groupings according to color ways and motif sizes, specially designed for quilting.

Rayon and polyester fabrics designed for clothing can be found in many pleasing colors and motifs.

These fabrics are available in the usual forty-five-inch widths, and they offer fiber content information and cleaning directions. Both rayon and polyester fabrics can mimic the feel and drape of silk. Many of these fabrics are beautiful, and they can be combined with vintage fabrics to create a fantastic ensemble.

These 100% cotton fabrics with Asian motifs are offered in groups by motifs and color ways. The motifs are of butterflies, koi fish, and dragonflies.

Two color ways of the same cherry blossom design in 100% cotton sateen.

These 100% cotton fabrics with large motifs can be cut, placed on a vest, and embellished with free-motion.

Hand-painted fabrics

Hand-painted fabrics are great, because they can be custom made to coordinate with whatever is already at hand. Look to vintage fabrics for unusual color combinations. Add carefully hand-painted motifs or scrunch and twist the fabric in a random manner and splash on dyes for an abstract design. When your fabric is unfolded, sometimes one end of the fabric will have a totally different blending of colors than the other end. Don't worry about an exact match of color. In fact, use this opportunity to add colors that will enhance what you already have.

Paint over existing fabric. Add bright color to disguise discoloration on vintage fabrics. Add a motif with a stencil or a stamp to enhance your work.

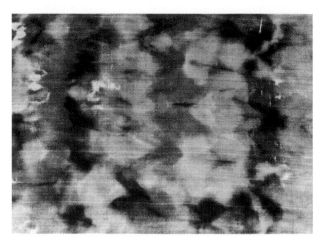

This fabric is hand painted using just black and yellow dyes. It is scrunched in a methodical manner, which created rows of color. This fabric is a sheer silk lining from an old kimono.

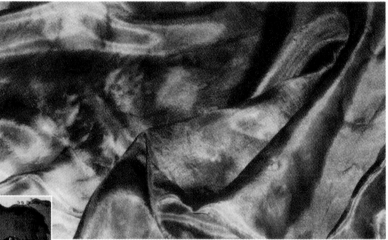

This fabric is hand painted with turquoise and magenta dyes and then scrunched in a random manner.

Detailed, hand-painted motif on a vintage kimono.

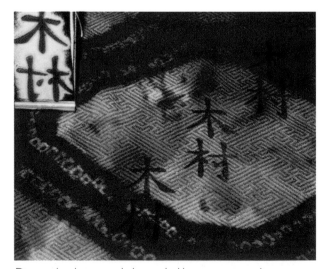

Disguise discoloration with dyes, and add your signature with a custom rubber stamp.

Silks

Dupioni silk in a solid color is a great companion to vintage Asian silks and blends. This silk shimmers and has wonderful slubs of texture. It lays flat and is easy to work with. It comes in several weights and in every color imaginable. This fabric needs to be dry-cleaned.

Crepe de Chine silk is a great fabric for painting. This silk is a durable and lustrous fabric with a fine, pebbly texture. It accepts smooth lines of color because of its weave. This silk can be washed and dried before painting and sewing. (Use Synthrapol®, a detergent without alkali. Alkali damages the fiber and reduces the luster.) Then, technically, it becomes a "wash and wear" fabric, but dry-clean the garment to reduce the fading of color and the twisting of specialty threads and batting.

Try to use a mixture of vintage and contemporary fabrics. If you have a stash of vintage fabrics, this is the time to use them. If you need more, there are several sources listed in the resource section of this book. Many of the vendors can be found at quilt shows, where each piece can be examined for rarity, condition, design, and color. Whole kimono are available as are smaller pieces from kimono that have been taken apart. Quilt shops now offer contemporary fabrics in prints and matching solids that have Asian motifs in traditional colors. These fabrics blend well with vintage fabrics. Or if you prefer using just solid color fabrics, the motifs alone lend Asian flair to any garment.

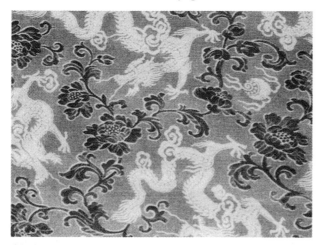

Silk chiffon with dragons and peonies.

Batting

Lightweight batting is used for vests and jackets even in a warmer climate. The batting allows the use of quilting techniques and helps to keep the attractive shape of the garment. If there will not be a lot of quilting on the garment, use a thin polyester batting, a layer of pre-shrunk flannel, or muslin. If there will be a consistent amount of quilting on the garment, use the polyester, cotton, or cotton blend batting that you prefer.

Contemporary fabric with Asian design.

Vintage kimono fabric with a bamboo design and a contemporary animal print.

Selecting color

Much of the color used in Asian textiles is determined by the seasons. Within each season are the plants that bloom, the color of the sky, the animals that appear, and the traditions that are celebrated. Colors were taken from nature to harmonize with the surroundings. Pastels and bright colors of spring and summer combined with flowers blooming at that time of the year are usually found together. Bright primary and secondary colors are used in textiles for children. Most of the festivals for children are held in the spring and summer. Darker and warmer colors are saved for fall and winter. Black is used for formal occasions.

The practice of changing colors, fabrics, and style for the seasons is also common in the United States. But our range of weather and use of travel no longer limit our wardrobe. Dark colors for winter can be worn in the evening all year. Light colors can be worn as resort wear. Art to wear is not limited by season, region, or time.

Festive primary colors found on the kimono of young girls reflect the mood of spring and summer.

Bright flowers for a special occasion.

Every color combination can be found in Asian textiles. There are certain combinations that are more prevalent—purple and green, aqua and pink, red and black, and blue and white.

Some colors are very predictable such as pink, red, orange, and green in a young girl's kimono. Blue, brown, and black are typical for a little boy's kimono. Then whimsy enters, and trees are not limited to green and brown, water is not limited to blues and greens, and cherry blossoms are no longer just pink. Every image can be tweaked to suit the fantasy.

A solution is to find a piece of Asian textile filled with colors, shapes, and motifs that is pleasing. Find a focal point, and then let your eyes flow to the next image. Make note of the images and colors. Determine how much of each color is used. Is it just used as an accent in small quantities, or is the same color used in different shades and mixed with other colors? You could also abandon all the analyzing, and use the colors that please you and match your wardrobe. Just a little bit gives you Asian flair.

A wintry scene of cool colors, fans, snow-topped pagodas, and dark, inky water.

Look carefully and you will notice the traditional use of green, purple, and orange in different shades.

Rusty orange and yellow-green are combined with gold.

A combination of red, black, and white.

Mystical creatures are orange.

Traditional use of blue, brown, and black in a boy's kimono.

Chrysanthemums and plum blossoms are colored blue to suit the design.

Purple, green, and orange.

Whimsical blue and red bamboo join flowers of the same colors.

Adding motifs

Many motifs used in Asian textiles were taken from nature and have symbolic meaning. Combined motifs can convey a story, show a rank or station in life, and tell the occasion for the textile.

Animals play an important part, whether they are real or part of mythology. Animals are used in the twelve-year cycle of the Chinese Zodiac, Chinese Fu Dogs have always guarded entryways, and dragons have always enjoyed popularity because the earliest Emperors of China claimed to have dragon's blood in their veins. The year 2000 was the year of the Dragon and created the availability of many contemporary fabrics with that image.

The lining of a man's kimono is depicted with large motifs encircling Fu Dogs.

The crane is the most popular bird with its sleek and noble demeanor. The crane represents a wish for longevity and is a popular motif on the Uchikake, a Japanese wedding kimono.

Flowers are used in abundance in every shape, color, and size. The cherry blossom is the most loved of the Japanese flowers. It is the national flower of Japan and connotes wealth and prosperity. When the cherry blossom blooms, winter is finally over. The iris is a flower that blooms in May and is usually depicted with water. The plum blossom blooms with the snow and stands for longevity. The lovely peony represents pros-

Overlapping "vignettes" of Mt. Fuji, pine trees, hexagons, and two beautiful cranes are found together.

The crane is highly embroidered with silver metallic threads and found on a red Uchikake.

perity, happy marriage, and joy. The lotus flower reminds us of absolute purity of the mind. The chrysanthemum was used as the Imperial flower. Its stylized image resembles the sun, which represents Japan.

The bamboo is revered for its strength and is used as an auspicious symbol. The beauty of the bamboo is reason enough for its frequent use. The unchanging pine also represents longevity and stamina.

Fans were a sign of refinement and an object of status. The noshi appears

Family crest. Found on formal wear.

today as a bundle of ornate ribbons tied together. It was originally a generous bundle of abalone and used as an offering to the gods.

Another good source for motifs are Japanese family crests. These are used on formal kimono. The family crest motifs are simple enough to be embroidered or stenciled onto a kimono. Some are encased in a circle. They can be enlarged and used as they are, or just a portion of their design can be used, since they sometimes have a repeat of the same image in a circular fashion.

Chrysanthemums of vibrant colors are in the foreground. Swirling waters can be seen in the jacquard weave.

These motifs include bamboo, gold embroidered peonies, chrysanthemums, and shibori clouds.

These peonies are ideal for embellishment.

When selecting and arranging the placement of the motifs, consider the size, the color, and the number of motifs that are to be used. Most motifs convey a positive connotation and can be appreciated just for their beauty. A floral arrangement with water, depicted by swirling thread, would look great with light, bright colors. A monochromatic arrangement of motifs with black rayon thread on black dupioni silk would be elegant.

A large motif of a Noh dancer encased by a fan would make a striking appliqué.

Create the motifs with sewing techniques, or cut out motifs from Asian textiles and apply them with those same techniques. Keep the motif lines clear and simple.

Don't worry about symbolism and keeping the plants separate by season. Sometimes the information is useful, but create what appeals to you. Even the use of one motif is enough to create Asian flair.

When placing motifs, almost every combination is possible. These are just a few suggestions to keep in mind while designing the motifs for your garment:

※ Place most of the large motifs near the bottom or way up high, because the bust and underarm areas cause bending and wrinkling.

※ Vary large and small motifs.

※ Vary the satin stitch widths.

※ Use a wider stitch width for items appearing closer.

※ Place large motifs (like the serene waters) on the fabric first, and then add smaller motifs (like the flowers and pine trees).

※ For large areas without motifs, add subtle designs using thread the same color as the jacket. This will create subtle "vignettes" and movement to another area of the jacket.

※ Highly embellished motifs should be prepared separately and then applied to the jacket.

Prancing horses with clear, simple lines can be cut and placed on solid fabric.

Adding texture

Use metallic and rayon threads in combination with satin stitch and free-motion techniques to mimic embroidery used on Asian textiles.

Vintage textiles embroidered with silk threads. The motifs include a crane, pine trees, bridge, and chrysanthemums.

Decorative threads

Threads are available in many colors, several weights, and vary in fiber content. Thread that is thicker can cover an area quickly while creating a raised texture. Thread that is thinner is wonderful for blending and creating a flatter texture.

Rayon threads give the luster and look of silk threads. They work well on all fabrics, are conducive to most sewing techniques, and are appealing in any design. Rayon threads are available in two weights. The 40-weight is a thinner thread and is available in a greater range of colors. The 30-weight is thicker and is available in almost as many colors. The 30-weight thread is ideal when used with dupioni

Sulky 30-weight rayon threads on large spools.

silk, because it adds to the lustrous slubs, characteristic of the fabric. These wonderful threads easily mimic the ancient, hand-embroidered designs on vintage textiles.

Metallic threads are exciting because they create drama, and the glitter attracts attention.

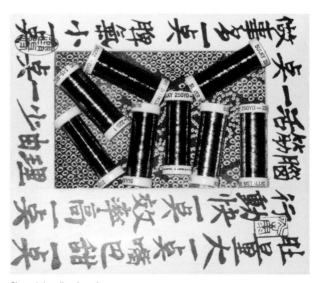

Sliver Metallic threads.

The metallic threads are associated with royalty, high cost, and a special occasion. Metallic threads can be found from gossamer-thin Sulky Sliver™ Metallics to twisted ropes with metallic slubs. They are versatile and result in a variety of textures when teamed with different application techniques. Metallic threads may require a special needle, a little tension adjustment, and a little help from a silicone lubricant (if your machine can tolerate it), but they are well worth the effort.

Superior Threads Glitter threads.

A mixture of rayon and metallic threads will allow you to be even more creative and to exercise control over what is to be emphasized. Use similar colors in rayon and metallic side by side to subtly shade, or use contrasting colors to highlight. Sometimes just a single line of metallic thread outlining a flower is all that is needed. Try all the threads on a small sewing project (such as Practicing sewing techniques on page 40) to see what appeals to you.

Needles

Selecting a needle for free-motion or the appliqué stitch will require a bit of testing. Take into account the type of fabric, the thickness of your fabric and batting, and the type of thread to be used. Metallic thread tends to fray and will require an appropriate metallic needle.

Embroidery needles work well for rayon threads. Quilting and denim needles are ideal for sewing through thick layers of fabric. Check with your local store, since new products are always coming on the market. Make sure to purchase enough needles, as you will have to change them frequently.

Stabilizer

Stabilizers are placed under fabrics for decorative stitching to promote even stitching and avoid puckering. Some stabilizers may be left in, but the majority must be removed after stitching. Ease of removal is important to avoid the pulling of delicate threads in an intricate design.

To eliminate puckering of the fabric, stabilizers and/or backing material (such as muslin or flannel) are needed when using the free-motion and satin stitch techniques. When batting is included, the stitches need to anchor onto something stable, so a backing material is needed. Inexpensive muslin or flannel can be used when there will be a layer of lining fabric to cover the backing material. If a very lightweight backing is needed, the Soft 'n Sheer stabilizer is ideal and made of non-woven nylon with stretch resistance to avoid pulling or sagging during stitching. This stabilizer can be used as a backing material. It can be left in the garment, and the excess can be cut away.

A crisper stabilizer, in addition to a backing material, is usually needed when satin stitching. The tight zigzag stitching can draw up the fabric and cause puckering. The weight of your fabric and the amount of stitching will dictate what kind of stabilizer you will need. Tear Easy™ is a crisp, lightweight stabilizer with effortless removal. Instead of purchasing a variety of stabilizers in different weights, Tear Easy can be layered to accommodate different fabric weights. Then removal can be done layer by layer to avoid the pulling of stitches. A removable stabilizer is usually not required with free-motion.

Free-motion

Free-motion is a versatile technique. It can be a utility stitch used to quilt layers of fabric and batting together with an artful design. It can also be an embellishing stitch to enhance with delicate lines or emphasize with many lines of stitching. Free-motion used with batting achieves a quilted look. Even without the use of batting, free-motion usually requires some kind of backing such as muslin, flannel, or stabilizer.

Free-motion is accomplished with the use of a darning foot or free-motion foot. The feed dogs are dropped when using the darning foot. And with the presser foot down, there is still enough space between the bottom of the foot and the throat plate to allow your fabric to move freely in any direction.

Contemporary quilted cotton fabrics can be embellished with metallic threads.

The needle is set to a straight stitch, and the stitch length is set to a normal setting. The stitch length will be determined by the speed of the needle moving up and down and how fast you move the fabric with your hands. This requires a little practice. Try making curves, loops, straight lines, and angles.

When you are starting in one direction and then returning in the opposite direction, be sure to place a few stitches at that end point before returning. (This will reduce broken needles and help keep the bobbin thread from coming up through the fabric.)

Start with your needle down, and stitch in place for a few stitches to lock the stitch. Keep the movement of your fabric and the speed of the needle consistent for even stitching. Music may help. (When you are adding free-motion to the two fronts of a vest, try to complete them together. Your rhythm can change from day to day.)

Some sewing machines produce the free-motion technique effortlessly, while other sewing machines are just incapable. If your machine has difficulty with free-motion, consider using a regular straight stitch with the appropriate settings while keeping your lines simple and angular.

Before you start, make a plan. Look at where you will start, what direction you will take, and where you will end. Sometimes a single line of stitching is enough, and sometimes going over the same length of stitching a few times will allow those lines to stand out above the others. Test these techniques to see if it creates the look you are trying to achieve.

Free-motion stitches in lines, side by side, can be used to create a shading technique. This requires a back and forth motion. The lines can be all the same length, or they can vary with short and long lengths. This is especially useful for shading flower petals. If you will be using a lot of free-motion all in one area, using a hoop will reduce the puckering and shrinking of that area. No matter how carefully you hold the fabric taut, there will be some minimal shrinking. (Be sure to allow for this when cutting your fabric.) Free-motion stitching eliminates the need for constant stopping and starting and for constantly cutting threads.

When you are using free-motion to outline

a motif such as flower petals, just retrace lines to create a bolder line. When using free-motion to outline the raw edge of a fabric, try to get as close to the edge as possible without shredding the weave. If it does shred, creating "eyelashes," use a sharp scissors and trim them off. (If your fabric is a loose weave, it may tend to fray. Use Dritz® Fray Check™ along the edges. First, test it on a scrap of fabric. If you apply too much, it will leave a dark mark.) Free-motion back and forth over the edge several times, until the edge of the fabric is covered with thread. To avoid breaking thread and needles, try to place each row of stitches closely together instead of on top of each other.

Satin Stitch

Satin stitch requires a zigzag or appliqué foot. An open toe at the front of the foot allows you to see the stitching. Make sure the bottom of the foot has an open channel to allow all the satin stitching to flow smoothly out the back. Set your machine to the satin stitch setting or to the zigzag stitch with a short stitch length. Even if your machine has a special setting, the stitch length can be adjusted. A shorter stitch length may be needed for a thinner thread, and a slightly longer stitch length may be needed for a thicker thread. Try different stitch lengths, and try all of the different widths. A small design or small curves will be accomplished more easily with a narrow width. A larger design will accommodate any width. The extent of the width will be determined by your machine make and model. Try it and see if you like the stitches as is, closer, looser, wider, or narrower. Be sure to record your preference of settings, since your machine may return to an automatic setting whenever it is turned on.

The width of the stitch can be changed at any time. Try changing the width while stitching. This can be used to create some interesting tapering effects.

Practice straight lines and wide curves. During a curve, make sure that the outside of the curve retains the same stitch length, while the inside of the curve will have stitches closer

and sometimes overlapping. Now sew smaller curves, such as for a petal. (Sometimes I use a little silicone lubricant such as Sew Easy™ and rub a drop on the throat plate to allow the fabric to glide easily.)

When creating a corner, sew to the end. For a left turn, swing your needle to the right side, and place your needle in the down position. Pivot the fabric. Start forward, going over the previous stitching. For a left turn, swing the needle to the left side, and place your needle in the down position. Pivot the fabric. Start forward, going over the previous stitching.

It takes some practice to create a "point," but it is worth accomplishing. It will require tapering the width to a straight stitch while in motion. Some machines will allow the needle to be placed in the left position with just the right side of the stitch tapering. When the needle is moved to the right side, just the left side of the stitch tapers. This is an incredible tool for mitering a corner.

Two simple sewing techniques, free-motion and the satin stitch, and a little creativity allow you to re-create ancient techniques as well as invent new ones.

Practicing sewing techniques

Textured eyeglass case

Free-motion and satin stitching are two basic techniques that create works of art, even when used alone. Before starting a large project, it is a good idea to assemble the supplies that will be used and to test them.

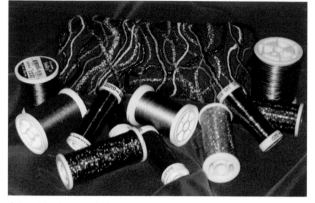

Select threads in colors that please you.

Sometimes the most beautiful thread gets lost in a fabric with the free-motion technique. When the same thread is used with the satin stitch, it comes to life. Then again, a flat metallic thread used with free-motion may be all that is needed for a subtle sparkle. When rayon thread is placed next to metallic thread, the contrast is complemented.

Make a test swatch with the fabric and threads to be used in the project. If the combination of fabric and threads is awful, throw it away and start over. At least the damage was small. If the combination of fabric and threads

Supplies

❋ Fabric: 10" x 10"
❋ Lightweight batting: Two pieces of 10" x 10"
❋ Backing fabric (muslin): 10" x 10"
❋ Lining fabric: 10" x 10"
❋ Threads: Rayon and metallic
❋ Practice sheet of lines
❋ Eyeglass case pattern

Sewing Techniques
Free-motion and satin stitching

is pleasing, use it to create an eyeglass case. Then you will have a matching accessory for your new project.

1. Trace the practice lines from page 125 onto the square of fabric. If your fabric is dark, and you are unable to trace through the fabric, trace the practice lines onto a lightweight tear-away stabilizer. Place the tear-away on the dark fabric, and trace the lines using a dark marker. The lines will seep through the tear-away and mark the fabric.

2. Use these lines to practice the free-motion and satin stitch techniques. Once you feel comfortable with the techniques, then meander, create curves, loops, angles, and corners on your own. See how each thread performs these techniques.

3. Place the fabric with the traced lines over a layer of batting, and then place these two layers over the backing fabric. Pin all of the layers together in a few places.

Layers of fabric, batting, and Soft 'n Sheer.

Glitter™, a hologram thread, is used with the free-motion technique.

4. Thread your machine with a decorative thread.

5. Set up your machine for free-motion with the appropriate foot attachment. Drop the feed dogs if using a darning foot. Some new free-motion foot attachments require the feed dogs in the up position.

6. Place your layers of fabric under the free-motion foot and start sewing at the left side of the practice lines. Place your hands several inches away from the foot, holding the fabric taut.

7. Slide the fabric with your hands to create the stitch length. Press the sewing machine pedal, keeping a steady pace. Move the fabric slowly to see how tight the stitches are, and then move the fabric quickly to see how long the stitches become. Sometimes if the stitches are too long, they will pucker the fabric. (This is not always bad. It can be turned into a creative technique.)

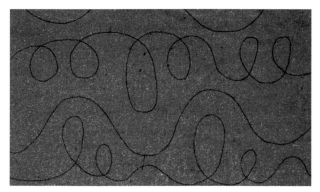

The lines are transferred from the practice sheet.

8. One of the advantages of free-motion is the fact that you don't need to turn the fabric to accommodate the sewing direction. The reason for practicing the loops is to see that the fabric is kept in the same position while moving it north, south, east, and west. The circular motion is similar to waxing a table. The cloth stays stationary under your hand while making a circular motion.

9. Change the threads, and make notes about the characteristics of each thread, such as the ease of use, if a specialty needle is needed, and whether the tension needed adjustment.

10. Set your machine for satin stitching with the appropriate foot. Adjust for a medium

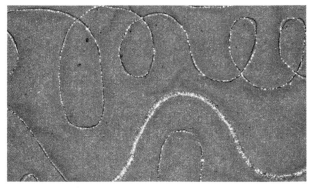

Some of the free-motion lines are used as guidelines for the satin stitching exercise.

width and appropriate stitch length.

11. Use the free-motion stitching as a guideline. Sew at a steady pace, and change the width while in motion. See how the stitches look from wide to narrow. This will be important when creating points. Experiment with the stitch length, if your machine allows.

12. Unlike free-motion, the fabric must be turned to accommodate the direction of the sewing. Learn to turn quickly for sharp curves and slowly for wide curves.

13. Experiment with sewing squiggly rows of thread side by side to see what is pleasing. Use colors that are similar, colors that contrast, and different types of thread.

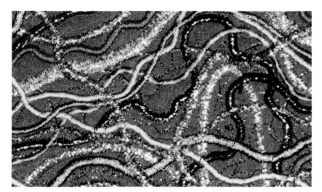

More thread is added.

14. When finished, cover the fabric with a pressing cloth, and press with the appropriate setting for the fabric.

15. Use the pattern provided on page 125 to cut the embellished fabric, another layer of lightweight batting, and the lining. Place the lightweight batting behind the embellished fabric, and treat it as one piece.

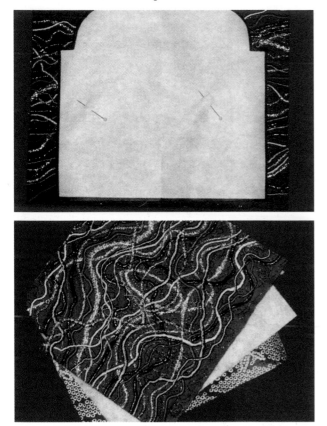

The eyeglass case pattern is used to cut the embellished fabric, batting, and lining.

16. Place the lining and embellished fabric with right sides together. Sew across the top with a 1/4" seam.

17. Trim the fabric, and clip the curves. Turn the lining so that the right side of the lining and the embellished fabric is facing out.

18. Fold the embellished fabric in half with right sides together. Sew the side and bottom with a 1/4" seam.

19. Trim the fabric. Finish the edges by serging, or use a zigzag stitch.

20. Turn the embellished fabric inside out, cover it with a pressing cloth, and press.

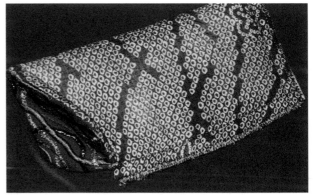

The eyeglass case just before turning the right side out.

21. Add dangling beads, using a variation of the stop stitch (next page).

Completed eyeglass case.

Adding embellishment

Beads add excitement to a garment. A few beads can be scattered about or placed purposefully in the center of a flower. For real drama, an image can be filled or outlined in beads.

Beads come in an array of sizes, shapes, and colors. Each bead sparkles in a different way. The sparkle can be anywhere from subtle to show stopping.

Bugle beads are long and tubular. This must be taken into consideration when outlining or creating a curved line.

Round beads come in many sizes and styles. These are usually very subtle and can be manipulated to form any kind of line. They can fill in areas perfectly or be used singly.

Plastic and metallic sequins are lightweight and faceted to reflect light. Crystal and glass sequins are spectacular, and their sparkle can be seen at a distance.

Rhinestones look great from a distance and up close. The glass stone is faceted and usually encased with metal and held together with prongs. There are holes in the metal casement for needle and thread to pass. Rhinestones can be found strung together or singly.

Beads and pearls can be used like the sequins or added to a tassel. They can be used as closures, to dangle off the end of a fan, or to accent an area. Use different sizes and shapes, and stagger the lengths of beads in the tassel for

Round-faceted Swarovski crystals are sewn to the face of the dragon. The flames are outlined and filled in with bugle beads.

An embellished tassel.

Round beads can be used in the center of the flowers.

The Creative Process   **43**

an unusual, untamed appearance.

Beads and sequins can be applied in many ways. Beading needles come in different lengths and sizes. When the needle is threaded, it must be able to go through the bead, sometimes several times. Beading threads come in all colors and thicknesses. And they are made of different materials. Pre-waxed, twisted nylon threads are available in many colors and work well with most beads. This thread is treated to resist being cut by the sharp edges of a bead. A hoop will help to keep the fabric taut.

One of the simplest methods of hand beading is the basic backstitch. The thread is knotted and sent up from underneath the fabric. The needle and thread pass through the bead or beads and back down through the fabric. To ensure stability, sew through the bead or several beads again before continuing.

The stop stitch can be used to secure

Strands of beautiful bugle beads

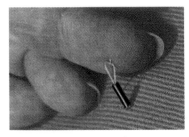

Tie a knot in the thread and send the needle up through the fabric and through the bugle bead.

Knotted silk cords create beautiful tassels.

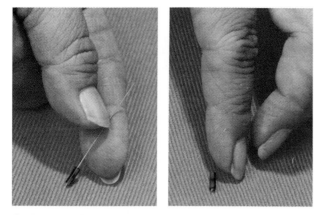

Send the needle back down through the fabric and repeat the steps sewing through the same bead once more with a backstitch to secure the beads.

Go back through the beads, several at a time, and then back through the fabric.

sequins or large beads placed singly. The thread is knotted and sent up from the bottom of the fabric. The needle and thread are sent through the center of the sequin or bead and then through a smaller bead. The needle is then sent back through the center of the first sequin or bead and back down to the back of the fabric. Tie a knot to secure the bead.

A variation of this stitch can be used to create tassels or to dangle beads. Use the stop-stitch procedure, but string the thread through six beads, add a small bead, then go back through the six beads and back through the fabric.

Dab a bit of Fray Check to keep the knots secure. Only a few basic methods and materials are covered that are relevant to the projects in this book. I encourage you to take beading classes and explore the vast array of the bead world.

Beautiful embellishments can be found. There are carved stones, fresh water pearls, fish carved from faux bone, Chinese calligraphy carved from mother-of-pearl, carved wooden beads depicting all the animals in the Chinese Zodiac, and metal charms.

Chapter 3

Art to Wear Projects

Lotus Purse

The lotus purse, like the lotus flower, is a round little blossom ready to burst into bloom and reveal an explosion of color. The beauty of this purse is in its simplicity of form. The lotus flower represents creative power, purity, and enlightenment.

This purse is created with one pattern piece, a little bit of fabric, and some rayon cord. It can be made quickly, or it can be ornately embellished with your creative powers.

Supplies

- ❊ Vintage fabric: Two pieces size 20" x 10"
- ❊ Lining: Two pieces size 20" x 10"
- ❊ Batting: Two pieces size 20" x 10"
- ❊ Rayon cord: 6 yards
- ❊ Decorative threads

- ❊ Sewing thread of matching color to assemble purse
- ❊ Needle: size 70 or 80
- ❊ Spray adhesive

- ❊ Soft 'n Sheer stabilizer: Two pieces 20" x 10"
- ❊ Typical sewing notions, including rotary cutter, mat, ruler, scissors, and pins
- ❊ Machine with free-motion foot

Sewing technique: Free-motion

Pattern

1. Use the pattern provided on page 108. Enlarge it 200%.

2. You will need two copies of the pattern. The first copy will be the original pattern. The second copy will need a 1/4" added around the perimeter of the pattern to account for the shrinkage that occurs with decorative stitching.

Cutting

1. Using the second copy of the pattern (with the 1/4" around the perimeter), cut two fabrics for the outside of the purse. Use the same pattern, and cut two of the batting, and two of the stabilizer.

2. Use the original pattern to cut two pieces of fabric for the lining.

Fabric and motifs

The beauty of the lotus flower can be found in its simplicity of line and color. As a bud, the outer petals display an inscrutable hint of pigment while keeping you in suspense. When finally in bloom, the softly curved petals and delicate shades of color inspire you to create an everlasting lotus flower that captures the essence of the moment.

Capture the colors and motifs for your special *Lotus Purse.* Find prints that are not too large. Place the pattern of the purse over the printed fabric, and imagine the size while gathering up the top edge with your fingers into little pleats (as the purse will be drawn closed). Are the motifs distorted or does it offer a wonderful abstract form of colors and line?

You can also create your own motifs. This gives you more control over the placement of the designs. Start with a solid color of fabric for your *Lotus Purse,* and select specific motifs and placement. Or add motifs to a printed fabric.

When selecting your lining for the purse, take the time to find something wonderful. Every time you open your purse, your flower will be blooming. Select a beautiful solid color, or add excitement with another print.

Here's a surprise. When you are finished, your purse will be reversible.

The original piece of vintage kimono fabric used to create the Lotus Purse.

Place the pattern on the fabric where you can best capture a motif. It is the bottom half of the purse that will show off a design. The top half of the purse will be gathered up with the loops and a cord strap.

Select a fabric with the motif placed close to the bottom of the purse.

This fabric is used on the other side of the purse.

Cording

1. Cut two strips of cord, each two yards long.

2. Knot the ends to avoid fraying.

Knot the ends before cutting to avoid fraying the cord.

3. Set the cord aside.

4. Cut 14 strips 4 1/2" long for the loops. To avoid fraying, measure the 4 1/2", and place a small piece of tape around the cord. Cut through the tape. Repeat. Set aside.

Preliminary assembling

1. Lightly coat both sides of the batting with adhesive spray.

2. Place the batting on top of the stabilizer. Smooth and press the stabilizer with your hands.

3. Place the vintage fabric on the batting. Smooth and press the batting with your hands.

4. Pin in several places.

Layer the pieces in this manner: Fabric, batting, and stabilizer.

Free-motion with decorative threads

1. Use a flat, metallic thread to bring shine to the motifs. If there is already a lot of gold in the design, consider an opalescent color or Sliver Metallic. It will create a pleasing contrast to the gold, instead of getting lost with the existing gold.

2. Use free-motion (see page 38) to outline the main motif. For example, outline the petals of a flower and the leaves. Select a few items on various parts of the purse, and embellish the items with decorative free-motion, at the same time anchoring all the layers together.

3. Add beading and other techniques.

4. When you are finished, re-cut each piece, using the original pattern as a guide.

Sliver Metallic thread is used to outline the crane and define the feathers.

Assembling

1. Place the two embellished pieces with right sides together.

2. Sew the sides and bottom with a 1/2" seam allowance.

3. Trim excess batting and stabilizer. Clip the curves right up to the seam line. Be careful not to cut through the seam line.

4. Turn right side out.

5. Place the two lining pieces with right sides together.

The fabric for the bag is sewn, clipped, and turned right side out. The lining is ready to be attached, and the rayon cord loops have been basted in place.

6. Sew the sides and curve, but leave a 5" opening at the bottom. Clip the curves right up to the seam line.

7. Place seven loops on each side, across the top of the embellished piece. Place them as indicated on the pattern.

8. Using a straight stitch, sew the loops in place 1/2" from the edge. Place the embellished piece and the lining with right sides together.

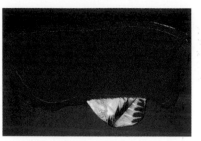

The fabric and lining have been sewn together across the top. The purse is ready to be turned right side out.

9. Pin at each side seam and around the top of the purse.

10. Sew the embellished piece to the lining with a 1/2" seam.

11. Trim the excess fabric.

12. Pull the embellished part of the purse through the hole in the bottom of the lining.

13. Tuck the lining inside the purse, and press. Be careful not to press the loops.

14. Use a blind stitch to close the seam at the bottom of the purse.

The purse has been pulled with the right side out, and the lining is tucked inside the purse.

15. Starting at one side of the purse, weave one cord through the loops.

16. Continue around the top, coming back to where you started.

17. Place the two ends of the cord together, and tie a knot 7" from the ends. (Extend or shorten this amount depending on how long the straps need to be for your height.) Start at the other end of the purse, and repeat the procedure.

18. To make sure the purse draws up evenly, pull each strap at the tied ends. When placed on your shoulder, the ends should dangle like a tassel.

The rayon cord straps are laced through the loops and tied in a knot.

Fabric from a boys under-kimono with motifs of horses in blues and browns is mixed with blue silk dupioni. The fabrics are embellished with blue rayon thread and satin stitching.

The reverse side of the obi is used for this orange and gold purse.

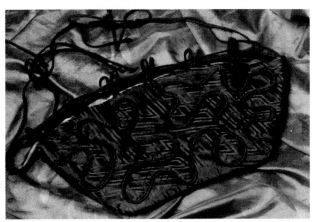

Fabric from a black obi is decorated with the same rayon cord as used for the loops and straps.

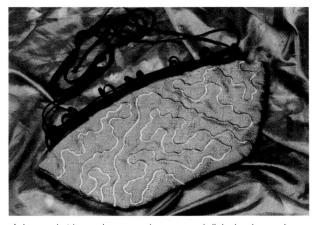

A brown obi fabric with a jacquard weave is embellished with meandering rayon thread in a similar color.

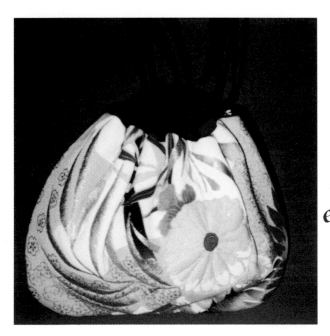

You are on your way to enlightenment!

This vest uses the traditional Japanese color combination of purple (murasaki) and green (midori) with contemporary cotton fabrics printed with Asian designs. These flowers are for an Empress, so a main fabric printed with gold is selected, and the flowers are embellished with gold thread. The cranes (representing longevity) and the color purple (saved for nobility) are a tribute to the Empress. The flowers and leaves are arranged in an asymmetrical and irregular manner as usually found in nature. Free-motion is the main sewing application, and hand beading finishes the garment.

Supplies

❀ Pattern: The Kimono Vest© by Kimura (Listings for alternate patterns are located in the resource section.)
❀ Main print cotton fabric: Enough for the vest and the lining
❀ Two coordinating cotton fabrics in solid colors

❀ Fabrics with Asian inspired motifs
❀ Lightweight batting
❀ Muslin (pre-wash and press)
❀ Iron-on interfacing
❀ Sewing thread that matches the fabrics to assemble the garment
❀ Decorative threads: Metallic and rayon

❀ Needle: Specialty, size 80 or 90
❀ Spray adhesive
❀ Beads
❀ Typical notions, including rotary cutter, mat, ruler, scissors, and pins
❀ Sewing machine with free-motion foot

This vest requires a main print with two solids (or prints with subtle designs). Other supporting fabrics with floral motifs are also needed. The vest is a simplified version of the kimono. The traditional neckband is pieced with two solid fabrics to accent the vest.

Throughout the project, you may use whatever colors you prefer. I will refer to the colors used in the sample photos.

Pre-wash your fabrics if you plan to hand wash your garment. I usually do not pre-wash the fabrics, because I like the original luster of the fabrics and intend to dry-clean the garment to avoid shrinkage and distortion of the surface design.

Pattern

1. Check the pattern, and make sure it fits. Allow for ease.

2. You will need two sets of patterns. The first set will be the original pattern, and will be used later to cut the lining pieces.

3. For the second set of patterns, make two copies of the front and add a 1/4" around the perimeter to account for the shrinkage that occurs with decorative stitching. While the two fronts are still placed together, draw a line from the front of the armhole down to the hem. Cut along this line.

4. Place all the front pattern pieces as they will be assembled, and label each piece.

5. Place the original back pattern on paper that is folded in half. Place the center back of the pattern on the fold. Add a 1/4" around the perimeter but NOT down the center back. (By making a second set back on the fold, you will be making a full back pattern.) While the back pattern is still folded in half, start at the armhole and draw a diagonal line downward toward the fold at the center of the back. Cut along this line. When unfolded, there will be a "V" shape for the upper back.

6. Cut an asymmetrical center back line.

7. Place all the back pattern pieces as they will be assembled and label each piece.

8. Lay out any fabric you have with the usual width (45"). Use this fabric as a guide to lay out the pattern pieces and determine how much of each fabric you will need. Add the amount needed for the lining to the amount needed for the main print. Add a 1/4 yard to each of the solids to allow for the pieced collar.

9. The first set of patterns will be used to re-cut the fronts and back after all the decorative stitching and embellishments are complete.

This is how the pattern should look. The two front patterns are identical and used with different fabrics. Create a softly curving line from the front of the underarm down to the hem. The upper back is cut in a "V" and the lower back is cut with a soft, asymmetrical curve.

Select a supporting fabric with large motifs and distinct lines. Use flowers that show up well on your fabric.

Fabric

1. Select a main print. The main print should have two or more colors.

2. Select two colors from the main print and use them as solids (or use prints with subtle designs that appear as solids from a short distance). The example uses purple and green as the two solids.

3. The main print should also be used for the lining, because this is a reversible vest.

4. Add at least one supporting fabric with large motifs. Select motifs with simple, distinct lines to cut.

5. Use fabrics with colors that will stand out from the main print and two solids. Florals are easy to work with and are easy to find.

Cutting

1. For the collar, cut 10 strips of purple fabric 1 1/2" wide and 16" long. Cut 10 strips of green fabric 1 1/2" wide and 16" long. Cut 2 pieces of iron-on interfacing 2 1/2" wide and 28" long. (The finished collar is 27" long. Your collar can be made longer by adding more purple and green strips.)

2. From the main fabric, cut the upper back piece, adding 1/4" to the lower edge where it will meet the solid fabrics. Cut the center fronts, adding 1/4" to the side edges where they will meet the solid fabrics.

3. Cut two fronts and one back (on the fold) using the ORIGINAL pattern. This will serve as the lining, and makes the vest reversible.

4. Cut the front left side and the lower back left side out of purple fabric.

5. Cut the front right side and the lower back right side out of green.

6. Cut two fronts and one back (on the fold) out of both muslin and batting, using the ORIGINAL pattern and ADDING A 1/4" around the perimeter.

Motifs

Select motifs that vary in shape, size, and color. Flowers are great to work with, since they can be found in every size and color. Feel free to add other related motifs such as ribbons and butterflies. The motifs are just a decorative way to cover the area where the two fabrics are joined. When the motifs are of different shapes, sizes, and color, it

Cut close to but not on the motif line.

will not look like a "stripe" of motifs covering the straight line.

If you are unsuccessful in finding fabrics with motifs that will work for you, use the motif templates in chapter 5. These motifs can be changed in size, they can be layered one over the other to create a cluster, and you can have control over the colors.

If you are lucky enough to have a fabric store near you that has a good selection of cotton fabrics with Asian inspired motifs, buy half a yard or more of each, and see how they work together. Don't let the background of the fabric deter you, because the motifs will be cut out and placed on your vest. Look in your stash for butterflies, dragonflies, and special little creatures found near flowers.

1. Cut the motifs, varying the sizes and shapes. In fabrics with Asian design, flowers are usually depicted in bunches. They are easier to cut out if they are left in bunches.

2. When you have picked out as many large bunches as you will need, you can cut into the remaining bunches to add specific flowers, colors, and shapes. Cut along the outside edge of the motifs.

3. You will be using the free-motion stitch along the motif lines. Some motifs may be incomplete (such as half of a flower, hidden because of another flower) and can be covered with a leaf or another motif.

4. Find fabric with small flower buds or sprigs to stick out here and there. Arrange these as you would a vase of flowers.

5. Cut the motifs, and apply a light coat of spray adhesive on the back. This will allow you to arrange motifs and still make changes. Use a large motif or a few large flowers on the back where the main fabric comes to a "V."

6. Use smaller flowers next to the large ones for contrast. Sprinkle a few large flowers

Add small and medium-sized flowers, covering the areas where the fabrics meet.

Add large purple leaves on the main print and the green fabrics.

Add large green leaves on the purple fabric.

mixed with smaller flowers. Leave spaces in between to add leaves. Do the same for the fronts.

7. Copy the two leaf designs from page 109. You can vary the sizes if you like. The larger leaves are used on the back. The smaller leaves are used on the front because of the limited space.

8. Cut the leaves out of the two solid colors.

9. Apply a light coat of spray adhesive to the leaves. Place the leaves around the flowers, tucking the stems under the flowers. The leaves are used to accentuate the floral motifs. Use your own arrangement or follow my example.

Use flowers to cover where the fabrics meet at the front.

Preliminary assembling

1. Lay out the muslin pieces. Place the left front, then the back, then the right front next to each other.

2. Apply a light coating of spray adhesive to the muslin. Place the batting pieces over the muslin pieces.

3. Apply a light coating of spray adhesive to the batting.

4. Place the main fabrics down on the batting.

5. Place the solid fabrics on the batting and the main fabric, allowing for the fact that the main fabric pieces have that extra 1/4" that will be covered. Use the shape of the muslin and batting as your guide to make the top fabrics fit. Place a few pins. The spray adhesive will keep everything in place.

Free-motion with decorative threads

Free-motion (see page 38) is the only decorative machine technique used to embellish this vest. It gives all the edges a soft and consistent appearance. The decorative threads are used to create depth, dimension, and detail on the flowers and leaves. To create the most shine, a flat metallic thread can be used. Do a test to see how it looks.

When using free-motion,

Use free-motion to define the leaves. Echo the shape of the leaves with purple metallic threads.

slightly longer stitches show off more shine. (You may have to adjust the tension if the bobbin thread comes up above the surface of the fabric.) Gold is used to outline most the flowers.

The same gold thread is used in a meandering design in the main print. It gives a subtle sparkle to the main print, which already had gold printed in the fabric. Gold is also used in the green, making it glow. The same flat, metallic thread in a deep, rich purple is used on the purple marbled fabric and creates a hint of glitter. Rayon thread is used to

add color and dimension to some of the flowers. Using darker shades in the center of the flowers creates shading as seen in real flowers.

1. Start at the center of the back with the large flowers. Working on the back gives you a chance to get a feel and a rhythm for free-motion.

2. Using free-motion, outline the large flowers, meandering into the petals and centers of the flowers. A single line is fine for the preliminary sewing. Do not worry about covering all the lines. This is

Outline the flowers with gold metallic thread.

to get everything anchored down. In some places, this is all that may be required. You will be able to go back and add more free-motion lines to accentuate and create shading.

3. When finished with the center, move out to the sides and then down the center. You can cross over lines, you can trace lines, and you can miss lines. Here, there are no rules.

4. Use free-motion to anchor the leaves.

5. Run a stitch down the center of the leaf, branching out to the sides to create veins. Come back to the center, then continue down, creating veins until you reach the tip of the leaf.

6. From the tip of the leaf, outline one side of the leaf, heading back to the stem. Sew again over the center of the leaf to the tip and then up the other side of the leaf, heading back to the stem down the center of the leaf. Go around the perimeter of the leaf again. Go on to the next leaf.

7. Use free-motion stitching over the areas along the top and sides that surround the motifs. Echo the leaf shapes.

8. Continue using free-motion to echo the leaves until you have evenly filled the space surrounding the leaves.

9. To protect the embellished fabric, lightly press the back piece with a pressing cloth.

10. Take a few steps back, and look to see where you would like to add more thread. Go back and use several lines of free-motion to accentuate certain flowers and petals and catch lines that you missed.

11. To shade the petals, use metallic threads in the same color as the flower but in a darker shade.

12. Use rayon threads on the flowers that surround the ones that have been accented with metallic. The contrast is very pleasing to the eye.

13. If an extreme amount of thread will be concentrated in one area, consider using a small hoop.

14. For the front, use similar methods as used on the back.

15. Start at the top at the front of the armhole, and work your way down. Try to keep the fronts equal in the amount of thread and free-motion used.

16. Don't try to make the fronts identical. Keep it asymmetrical, as it is in nature.

17. Do the two fronts on the same day. Your rhythm for free-motion can change from day to day.

Using beads to embellish

Add beading to create a pleasing surprise where it is unexpected. On the back, your eyes will follow the shape of the motifs and the colors. Then your eyes will be drawn to the shiny threads. Your eyes are naturally drawn to the lighter color (green) embellished with the lighter (gold) metallic thread. The purple area appears quietly waiting to make its presence known, so a scattering of purple bugle beads is just enough to bring some subtle reflection to that area.

1. Arrange a few beads to see how close and at what angle they should be placed.

2. Thread a beading needle with waxed nylon thread, and use the basic backstitch.

3. Go through each bead two or three times, and knot underneath frequently.

4. Do the same for the purple area on the front.

Assembling the collar

This traditional collar is a simple band as found on all kimono. The band is usually two inches wide and can cross over the front or hang straight down, depending on the type of kimono. This collar instantly gives the garment an exotic Asian look. For this

Close up of the beading on the back.

Side view of the left front and left back with beading.

vest, the collar is modified with the piecing of two fabrics of different colors. This brings interest and balance to the front of the garment, while preserving the traditional shape.

1. For the collar, sew alternating strips of purple and green together. Start with a purple strip and end with a purple strip.

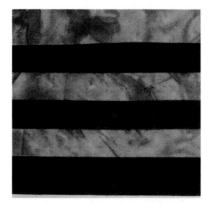

Sew alternating strips of green and purple.

2. Press the seams to one side, towards the darker fabric. Cut the strips into 5" pieces, and then sew them together into one long band.

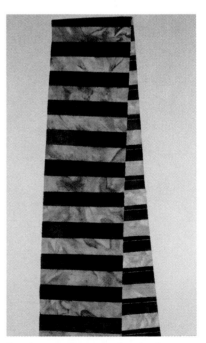

Sew the 5" pieces into one long band.

3. Measure the band to see if it is long enough or too long. Add a few more strips or take some off.

4. Fold the collar in half with the right side of the fabric facing out, and press.

5. Unfold the collar, and place the iron-on interfacing on one side. Press.

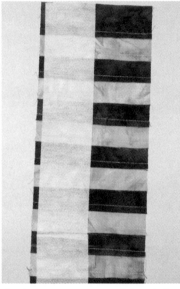

Apply the interfacing to one half of the band.

6. Fold the ends of the collar with the right sides of the fabric together. Sew a 1/4" seam, and turn right side out. Press.

Turn ends with the right sides together and sew.

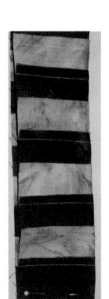

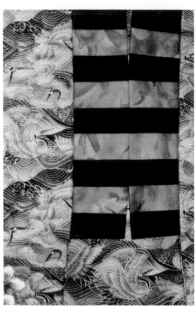

The band ends start and end with a purple strip.

Assembling the Vest

1. Place the original patterns over the embellished fronts and backs. Re-cut the embellished pieces back to the original shape.

2. Sew the embellished fronts and back with right sides together at the shoulder. Use whatever seam allowance is required on the pattern instructions.

3. Sew the lining fronts and back with right sides together at the shoulder.

4. Prepare the back neckline for the collar with a stay stitch and clipping. Do this for the lining and the embellished piece. Place the center of the collar at the center of the back neckline on the embel-

Stay stitch and clip the neckline before applying the collar.

lished piece. Pin evenly down each front and sew.

5. Place the embellished front/back and lining front/back with right sides together. Sew along all edges except side seams. Trim and clip at curves.

6. Pull each front through each shoulder and continue to pull together through one side seam. Smooth out and press.

7. To finish the side seams, place fronts and backs of the embellished sides together.

8. Pin armhole seams together.

9. Pin bottom seams together.

10. Line up the side seams and pin. Start sewing the seam before the pin at the armhole and end after the pin at the bottom.

11. Tuck the seam allowance under, and hand sew to close. Press.

Wear Your Vest Proudly.
You Are The Empress!

*T*he Maiko is the young apprentice Geisha known for being adorned with brilliantly colored and highly embroidered kimono. With its hand painted Asian motifs and satin stitching to emulate vintage hand embroidery, this vest is a tribute to the Maiko.

Jewel-toned fabrics are pieced together and embellished with decorative machine stitching, lustrous rayon, and metallic threads. A large motif is placed in an asymmetrical manner and embellished. The vest is finished with special detail given to the back when The Tsunami Vest© pattern is used.

Supplies

❋ Pattern: The Tsunami Vest© (check pattern for fabric requirements), or pattern of similar shape
❋ Paper to trace the pattern
❋ Various fat quarters of jewel-toned silks (select three to six)
❋ Bias binding (select one of the fabrics used for the front). 1/2-yard will be needed to create 15 feet of 2"-wide bias binding

❋ Silk fabric for the back, back lining, and front lining (Enough fabric to cut two back pieces and one set of fronts. You can use the same fabric as one of the fabrics used to piece the front.)
❋ Lightweight batting
❋ Sewing thread that matches the fabric to assemble the garment

❋ Decorative threads: Metallic and rayon
❋ Needle: Specialty or size 80
❋ Spray adhesive
❋ Tear-away stabilizer
❋ Typical notions, including rotary cutter, mat, ruler, scissors, and pins
❋ Sewing machine with free-motion foot and satin stitch foot

Sewing technique
Free-motion, satin stitch

(This vest should be dry-cleaned for best results)

Pattern

1. Check the pattern, and make sure it fits.

2. You will need two sets of patterns. The first set will be the original pattern.

3. The second set will need 1/4" added around the perimeter of the front and the perimeter of the back, but NOT down the center of the back. (A 1/4" must be added to the second set to account for a slight shrinkage that occurs with decorative free-motion stitching.)

4. The second set will require two fronts. Each front will be divided into three sections.

5. Make a note on your pattern to allow an extra 1/4" on both sides of the middle section of each front. Then when the three sections are placed together again, the top and bottom pieces will be placed over the middle piece so that the batting will not show through.

6. Place one of the front patterns so that the center of the vest faces left. This will be the left side of the vest so label it LEFT, and number the pieces from the top to the bottom: L1, L2, and L3.

7. Turn the other front pattern so the center of the vest faces right. Label this side RIGHT and number the pieces: R1, R2, and R3.

8. That middle piece can look nondescript once it is cut up, so it's best to also mark and label the center front with a notch before it's cut up.

9. The back on The Tsunami Vest is asymmetrical, but it will be treated as a plain back. The Tsunami wave will be cut out later, before the bias tape is applied.

Cut the pattern into three pieces. Use different fabrics.

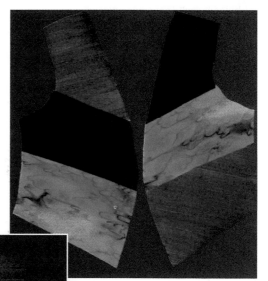

Place fabrics together, overlapping at the edges.

View of the back.

Fabric

Select a color scheme of three or more colors to use on the front of your vest. If you are using three fabrics, just alternate them in different sections, so they are not in the same place on both fronts. Select up to six fabrics if you wish. They can be monochromatic (differing shades of the same color). They can be complementary (colors found opposite of each other on the color wheel). They can be analogous (colors found next to each other on the color wheel). Or just use your favorite colors.

Some suggestions for types of fabric would be: Silk dupioni, silk Crepe de Chine, silk charmeuse, cotton sateen, rayon, and polyester. Mixing textures creates an interesting effect when using solid colors. (A vintage print would be a great replacement for the hand painted Geisha face in the fan shape.) Layout all the possibilities, and see how they look next to one another. Take note of the textures and colors. Make sure they are easy to work with.

Cottons work well, too. Use leftover fabrics from quilts you have made. This way all the color matching has already been done.

Don't hesitate to use rayons and polyesters as well. If you use fabrics that stretch, make sure to back them with iron-on interfacing that does not stretch.

Laces and trims, and certainly charms and trinkets, can be added. Little dragonfly

charms placed here and there would be an auspicious touch. Add simple beading, learned from the Embellishment section (page 43) and maybe a tassel for the fan.

Cutting

1. Lay out the fabric selected for the back, back lining, and front lining. Fold the fabric, placing right sides together.

2. Use the back from the second set of patterns (with the added 1/4"), and cut two backs. The center of the back is placed on the fold of the fabric.

3. Use the front from the second set of patterns (with

the added 1/4"), and cut one set of two front pieces.

4. Use the back from the second set of patterns to cut one back out of the batting.

5. Use the front from the second set of patterns to cut one set of two front pieces out of the batting.

6. Lay out the fabrics for the front with the right sides facing up.

7. Cut out the three sections for the left side and then for the right side. Label them, or place the fabrics as they will be sewn. Don't forget that the center piece has the notch to indicate the center front.

Motifs

Use rubber stamps and stencils to create motifs and prints on your fabric. They work best when the front pieces are pressed and cut out. The fabrics will be flat, and it will be easier to decide where to place the designs to accommodate the shape of the piece of fabric.

Use the same colors in different shades for a subtle, monochromatic look. Or try gold paints to make your designs stand out.

Stamp and stencil designs (see chapter 1), such as the meadering pine and chrysanthemum in water. Fans certainly add an air of refinement. See chapter 5 for more examples.

Erasable ink used in combination with the rubber stamps and stencils can be used to create guidelines for quilting later.

Chrysanthemum in water

Meandering pine

Geisha

The line drawing is placed under the silk as shown on the left. The lines are traced with a black fabric pen.

1. Place a 12" x 12" square of Crepe de Chine silk over the line drawing of the Geisha (see chapter 5).

2. Using a fabric pen, make quick and sweeping lines with a light touch on the fabric, and trace all the lines. (More ink from the pen will be released on the fabric when the pen moves slowly or when there is more pressure on the fabric. This will result in thick, bleeding lines.)

3. Press to heat set the fabric pen lines.

4. Stretch the silk on a frame or hoop.

5. Using a small, firm brush, apply resist outside of the lines that outline the Geisha's hair. This will keep the dyes or inks inside the lines.

6. Inside the area of her hair, carefully apply resist inside the lines of the comb and paintbrush tips. This will keep the black dye or ink from going into that area. The comb and brush tips will later be painted with color.

7. There are some brush tips protruding outside the area of her hair. Apply resist outside the lines of the paintbrush tips.

8. Apply resist outside the lines that outline the lower two layers of her kimono.

Apply resist with a small, firm brush for more control. The resist will keep the dyes and inks confined.

9. Use black dye or ink to paint her hair. Remember to use the appropriate brush techniques for the dye or ink (see chapter 1). Let dry completely.

10. Remove from the hoop, and place several layers of paper towel under the Geisha. Use quick touches with fabric pens to paint the small designs on the Geisha's kimono. Also paint the brush tips outside of the area of her hair. Let dry completely. Press to heat set the inks.

11. If you used dyes, immerse the fabric in a fixative bath, or use a brush to paint the fixative over the dyed areas. If painting the dyeset onto a specific area, apply dyeset while the fabric is in the hoop. Follow the preparation directions provided with the dyeset.

12. After the dyeset has been applied for the appropriate amount of time or the inks have been heatset, immerse the square of silk in water with a mild soap, and lightly rub until the resist is removed. Place the silk on a dry towel. Cover it with another towel, and press to remove as much moisture as possible. Lightly press between two pressing cloths.

13. Stretch the silk on a hoop or frame again. This time apply the resist inside the lines of the Geisha to keep the dyes and inks out. Apply resist in the hair area around the comb and paintbrush tips. Let dry completely.

14. Use dye or ink to paint the background around the Geisha face. Make sure to paint enough background to fill what will be the fan-shaped area. Use different dye or ink colors side by side, and let them blend, or use the Fantastix dipped in water to push the dyes and inks around and create a watercolor effect. Mix dye or ink colors in a separate dish and apply them with swirling strokes. If using inks, work quickly. Sprinkle salt while the colors are wet to create an interesting effect. Let the fabric dry completely.

15. Use dye or ink to paint the inside of the comb and paintbrush tips.

16. When dry, the fabric can be pressed to set the ink, or fixative can be applied to the dye. Remove the resist.

Preliminary assembling

1. Lay out the lining for the front with the right sides down and center fronts facing each other.

2. Apply a light coating of spray adhesive to both sides of the batting. Place the batting on top of the lining. Press and smooth out the lining with your hands.

3. Place the middle sections in the center of each front piece. Place the top sections above the middle sections. Place the bottom sections below the middle sections. You should have what looks like two complete front vest pieces. You will notice that the edges of the middle piece are slightly overlapped by the top and bottom. This is to keep the batting from showing.

4. Press and smooth out the fabrics with your hands. Cut strips of tear-away stabilizer, and place them under the area where the fabrics meet.

5. Use a loose basting stitch to keep all the layers in place.

6. Enlarge the fan shape so that the Geisha will fit inside. Place the fan shape over the Geisha face, and trace the perimeter. Make sure to get all of her in the fan. Cut along the fan's lines. Lightly spray the back of the fan-shaped fabric with spray adhesive just before placing it on the right vest front. See step 6 in the next section.

7. Lay out the lining for the back with the right side down.

8. Apply a light coating of spray adhesive on both sides of the batting. Place the batting on the lining. Press and smooth the lining with your hands. Place the back fabric over the batting, and smooth the fabric with your hands.

9. Place a few pins all over the back.

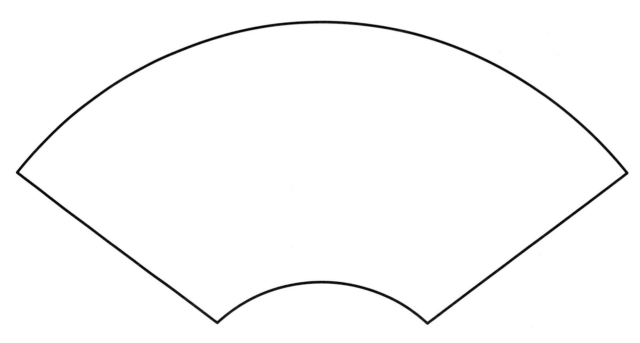

Enlarge the fan 225%, so that your Geisha face will fit inside. The sides of the fan may be altered to fit the garment.

Free-motion and satin stitch with decorative threads

1. Use the decorative machine stitches (see pages 38-39) to cover the areas on the front of the vest where the fabrics meet.

2. Use a large decorative stitch that incorporates the satin stitch technique to cover the raw edge of the fabrics.

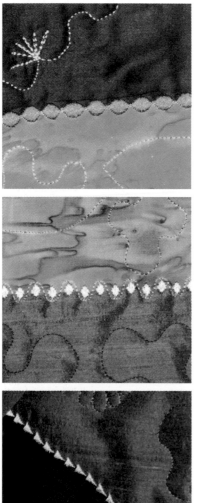

Use decorative stitching where the fabrics meet.

3. Test a few stitches using the recommended stitch length and width on a scrap of fabric. Get accustomed to feeding the fabric through your machine at a constant speed to ensure that the repeated designs are consistent.

4. See how the designs look in rayon and metallic threads. These stitches can be set to different sizes, programmed for a sequence of designs, and mirror imaged. They vary from big and bold to delicate and lacey. If your machine does not offer any machine embroider stitches, use lace or trim.

5. Remove the tear-away carefully.

6. Place the Geisha motif on the right front.

The Geisha face is placed on the right side of the jacket and on part of the bottom section.

7. Lay the Geisha face mostly on the middle section, spilling over to the bottom section.

8. Sew a straight stitch around the fan, close to the edge, because it will be covered with sating stitching. Use the same thread that you will use for the decorative stitch.

9. Use the straight stitch or free-motion stitch with black rayon thread to outline the Geisha's hair, face, and throat.

10. Cut a piece of tear-away stabilizer larger than the Geisha motif, and place it underneath the design. Pin in a few places.

11. Set your machine to satin stitch.

12. Use a narrow width satin stitch to outline the hair ornaments. The details are small, and it would be difficult to maneuver a wide satin stitch.

13. Use the same narrow width to outline some of the straight-line designs in the kimono.

14. Use a medium width to outline the layers of her kimono.

15. Use an even wider satin stitch to emphasize the shape of the fan.

16. Use free-motion to outline the finer details of the kimono after the tear-away stabilizer has been removed.

Assembling the Vest

1. Place the original front pattern over the embellished fronts. Re-cut the embellished fronts to match the original. Place the original back pattern over the quilted back. Re-cut the quilted back to match the original pattern.

2. If you are using The Tsunami Vest, cut out the asymmetrical wave on the back.

3. Prepare four pieces of chord to tie at the opening in the back: Cut four pieces of chord 14" long. To keep them from fraying, knot each of the ends. Place two chords on each side. Baste them into place.

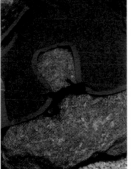

Place the cords in the seam.

4. Place the fronts and backs with right sides together. Sew at the shoulders and side seams.

5. Use a serger to finish the seams, or trim them, and use a zigzag stitch to finish the seams.

6. Press the side and shoulder seams toward the back.

7. The next step will be to finish the edges with bias strips.

Finish the side seams.

Adding the bias strips

These directions are brief. If using a rotary cutter for the first time, please be sure to observe a demonstration of the proper handling and positioning. Work slowly and carefully, keeping your hands away from the path of the rotary cutter.

1. Use your rotary cutter, mat, and ruler to create bias binding. Your mat will show a 45° angle to use in cutting fabric on the bias. Line your fabric up with the horizontal edge and find the correct angle/line. Line your ruler up with the line and cut with the rotary cutter.

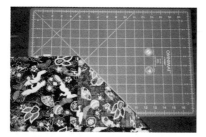

Line up the fabric on the mat.

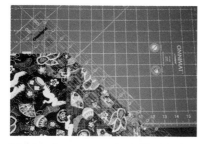

Use the ruler to measure the width of the bias strips.

2. From that edge, use your ruler to find the 2" increment and cut strips. (The 2" bias strip width is determined by the fact that my pattern calls for a 1/2" seam allowance. It takes four times the seam allowance to bind the edge. If you are using a narrower or wider seam binding, your bias strip will be a different width.) One half yard is a generous amount to cut approximately 15 feet of bias (you will need more or less depending on the pattern used), so please use long strips to avoid frequent joining of strips.

3. To join the strips, place them right sides together at a 90° angle.

4. Sew from inside corner to inside corner.

5. Press the strips open and trim.

Trim and press strips.

6. Press the strips in half with wrong sides together.

7. Start with the bottom end of the vest. Place the right side of the bias strip against the right side of the vest. Start this strip at the bottom of the right front.

8. Loosely, pin the strip heading toward the back, across the back, and to the left front.

9. Sew with a 1/2" seam allowance.

10. Turn the bias strip over the seam allowance, and tuck the edges under on the other side.

11. On the other side, place the tucked edges over the thread that shows from the previous seam. Pin.

12. Hand sew in place. Trim any excess fabric from the ends.

13. Apply the bias strip to the front and neck back. Start at the left front bottom edge and go up to the neck, around the neck, and down the right front. Place the right side of the bias strip against the right side of the vest, but with the end of the bias strip turned back a half inch. This way the raw edge of the fabric will not show.

14. Loosely, pin the strip and sew with a 1/2" seam allowance. Turn the bias strip over the seam allowance and tuck edges under on the other side.

15. On the other side, go up to the thread that shows from the previous seam. Pin. Hand sew in place.

16. Apply the bias strip to the armholes. Start at the bottom of the armhole. Turn back the beginning edge of the bias strip 1/2", and start at the side seam.

17. Place the right side of the bias strip against the right side of the vest edge. Pin.

18. Continue around the armhole until you arrive at the beginning. Overlap the beginning a 1/2". Sew around the armhole with a 1/2" seam allowance.

19. Clip the curves to the seam line. Turn the bias strip over the seam allowance, and tuck the edges under on the other side.

20. On the other side, place the tucked edge on the thread from the previous seam. Pin. Hand sew in place.

Now Celebrate!

Tomesode Jacket

This jacket is a tribute to the traditional tomesode (toe-may-so-day) kimono with its beautiful designs flowing along the length of the hem. A kuro (black) tomesode is a highly formal kimono, usually with family crests, worn by adult women. An iro (color) tomesode, also for special occasions, has a background color other than black. Another kimono of similar style is the tsukesage (tsoo-kay-sah-gay), with an asymmetrical pattern at the left shoulder and flowing pattern at the hem. The use of brilliantly beautiful motifs that run horizontally across the hem, rising slightly on the left overlapping front of the kimono, is a spectacular sight when surrounded by an expanse of solid black or a solid color. Since our modern jackets are not worn so long, the effect could not be transferred, but the beauty of the motifs can still be appreciated.

Supplies

- ❁ Pattern: The Self Collar and Cuff Jacket© by Kimura (Or choose a different pattern in a similar style. Remember that a dolman sleeve is easier to work with.)
- ❁ Solid color dupioni silk for the jacket, including a 1/2-yard for bias strips
- ❁ Lining for the jacket
- ❁ Vintage fabrics for motifs
- ❁ Small amounts of dupioni silks in various colors for motifs
- ❁ Thermore™ lightweight polyester batting for the jacket
- ❁ Soft 'n Sheer or lightweight muslin for the jacket and motifs
- ❁ Lightweight tear-away stabilizer
- ❁ Lightweight iron-on interfacing, a small piece for the Noshi
- ❁ Sewing thread that matches the fabric to assemble the jacket
- ❁ Decorative rayon and metallic threads
- ❁ Needles: Size 80 or 90, specialty needle for metallic thread
- ❁ Spray adhesive
- ❁ Fray Check
- ❁ Black rayon cording
- ❁ Typical notions, including rotary cutter, mat, and quilting ruler
- ❁ Sewing machine with free-motion and satin-stitch foot

Pattern

1. Check the pattern and make sure it fits. Use a pattern with dolman sleeves (the body and sleeve of the jacket are all in one pattern piece). Make alterations to the jacket and sleeve lengths at this time.

2. Make a muslin version of the pattern, remembering to allow for ease if you are unsure of the fit. (Take into account that these jackets usually require shoulder pads, and allow for ease in the shoulder and upper arm area.)

3. You will need two sets of patterns. The first set is the original. The second set will need 1/4" added around the perimeter (to account for a slight shrinkage that occurs with decorative free-motion stitching). Do not add the 1/4" to the center of the back.

Cutting

1. Press the dupioni silk to eliminate any wrinkles.

2. With the fabric open to its full width, fold it in half lengthwise with right sides together. The selvages should meet on the right and left sides. This will allow you to cut the large patterns all in one piece. Do the same for the batting and muslin. If you prefer a lighter weight jacket,

A formal wedding picture. Notice the beautiful motifs along the hem.

use the Soft 'n Sheer in place of the muslin. It comes on a roll or in cut sheets and needs to be pieced.

3. Do not sew the pieces of Soft 'n Sheer together. Just lay the sheets with edges meeting and pin.

4. Check your pattern instructions for the best pattern layout. Cut the lining from the original patterns.

5. Cut the dupioni silk, batting, and muslin from the second set of patterns (with the added 1/4").

Free-motion and satin stitch with decorative threads

A preliminary satin stitch (see page 39) is used to define the edges and keep them from fraying. This satin stitch will have a slightly longer stitch length and slightly narrower stitch width than a standard satin stitch. This technique can be used when stitching a motif on decorative fabric that will be cut close to the preliminary satin stitch and placed on the jacket. This is done with the understanding

Art to Wear Projects 73

that when the motif is applied to the jacket, the preliminary satin stitch will be covered with a standard satin stitch.

A preliminary straight stitch is the same as a regular straight stitch. It is used along the edge of a motif that is being applied to the jacket to anchor the motif. The preliminary stitch is later covered with a standard satin stitch. A preliminary straight stitch can also be used as a guideline to show where the decorative satin stitch will create the motif on the jacket.

Decorative threads

The 30-weight, solid-color rayon threads create a beautifully raised satin stitch, as well as enhance the free-motion designs. The variegated rayon threads can be used to create some interesting effects. Metallic thread is used sparingly to draw your eyes to specific motifs.

To add dimension to items in the foreground, add another layer of satin stitching.

Stabilizers

Use stabilizers under satin stitching to reduce shrinkage and puckering. Use a lightweight stabilizer for small and simple motifs. Use a medium to heavier weight stabilizer for projects that require a good deal of stitching. (Or use two layers of lightweight stabilizer.)

If there are several layers (such as dupioni silk, then batting, and then muslin), the stabilizer is still placed last. Tear-away stabilizer is the ideal choice for use with satin stitching, because it is easy to remove. After all the stitching is completed, remove the stabilizer.

If tear-away stabilizer is used under the free-motion, it can be difficult to remove without pulling or breaking threads. A good stabilizer for free-motion is the Soft 'n Sheer nylon that allows a natural look. Any excess can be cut away or left in. This is optional.

Motifs

Plan your motif placement (see Adding motifs, page 33). Make sure the motifs fit. Enlarge or shrink the designs to suit your pattern and size. Add more motifs, or use just one element of the design. (A great monochromatic look would be to use just the satin stitched fans on the right side of the jacket and just the free-motion waves on the left side.)

One of the easiest ways to apply the guidelines for the motifs directly onto the jacket fabric is by tracing. If your fabric is light in color, you can place the motifs underneath the jacket fabric and trace the lines. If your fabric is darker but not too thick, a light table will allow you to see the lines through your fabric. (A light table can be purchased, or a glass table top with a lamp placed underneath works well.)

A template can be used for simple shapes. Stencils can be used with erasable ink, pencil, or chalk pencil.

Some of the motifs are large and require a good deal of embellishing. The crane and peonies on the black jacket and the noshi and large waves on the back of the gold jacket are embellished with satin stitching and free-motion then attached to the jacket with satin stitching around the perimeter.

The smaller motifs are applied to the jacket with satin stitching, and details are added. Some motifs are created with just thread, directly on the jacket.

Any of the motifs that are created with just thread (such as the fans and small wave) are traced onto the jacket fabric. Outlines of the motifs can be placed on the jacket fabric with erasable ink to allow for easier placement later. If you change your mind, just erase the lines with a damp cloth.

Instead of tracing the feathery waves, it would be better to use free-motion through improvisation, after some practice. Meander the waves in a wandering line, leaving some space surrounding them. This allows you to see the exaggerated movement of each line of meandering wave as well as each feathery tip.

The feathery waves are created with free-motion and spaces that allow you to appreciate the curves and movement created.

For the gold jacket

Fans

1. The fans are placed on the right side of the jacket, including the sleeve.

2. Make a template of the fan. Place the fans askew, tilting them this way and that way.

3. Vary the distances between the fans.

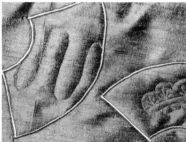

Turn fans to different angles.

4. Trace more fans going down the right arm. Do this on the right back and right front. Use the photo of the gold jacket as a guide.

5. Inside each fan, trace one of the simple motifs—bamboo, chrysanthemum, cherry blossoms, serene water, or pine trees—found in chapter 5. Shrink the size of these motifs to fit inside the shape of the fan. Create the motifs inside the fans with the free-motion technique.

Bamboo

The traditional design of a group of bamboo leaves placed in this manner is one that is seen repeatedly in fabric, in a family crest, and used by artists and craftsmen. The bamboo is placed inside the fans on the jacket and created with free-motion.

1. Start the free-motion at the top center of the left leaf. Follow the shape of the entire leaf counter clockwise back to the top, down the center, and back up to the top.

2. Continue on to the next leaf to the right, and repeat the method until all the leaves are completed.

3. You may have to go over existing stitching to get over to the next leaf. That is expected. When you are ending on the last leaf, stitch in place for a few stitches to anchor the thread.

Chrysanthemum

This is a stylized version of the chrysanthemum. It doesn't really look like the flower, but traditionally it's been depicted this way. This motif has come to represent the chrysanthemum and appropriately so, since it looks like the sun, the symbol of Japan. This motif is used on the right side of the jacket in the fan. It is created with free-motion.

1. Start the free-motion at the center circle. Stitch in place for a few stitches to anchor

the thread and then go up a petal and back down to the center circle.

2. Continue on with the next petal, using the same method.

3. When all the petals are completed and you are back to where you began, sew around the circle twice and then anchor the thread.

Noshi

The noshi is depicted as a bundle of ribbons in movement. It is given a placement of honor high up on the left shoulder. A variety of textures and colors are selected to magnify their merriment and dance. Starting at the right, an orange and gold ribbon is taken from an obi, and purple

dupioni is placed next to it for contrast. A ribbon of orange faux shibori is added for its raised texture and small print. The next ribbon is taken from a child's kimono with its brilliant primary colors and asymmetrical print. The last ribbon is lime green dupioni silk, embellished with a meandering of variegated rayon thread. (The machine is set for satin stitch, and it is a matter of nervously wiggling the fabric to create this design.)

1. Enlarge the noshi line drawing from page 114. (A smaller version could be used on the front of the jacket.)

2. Trace two copies of the drawing. Keep one intact.

3. Cut the second copy around the edges, eliminating the excess paper.

4. The second one should then be numbered and cut up. Mark the numbers and an F for front and B for back on each ribbon half.

5. Select five fabrics. Place your numbered pieces on each fabric and cut. Use one of the five fabrics, or select a new fabric for the band that holds all the ribbons together.

6. To add black rayon cording to the noshi, cut three or

Three black cords knotted at the ends.

more rayon chords, 18" long. Tie the ends into a knot to stop them from fraying. Set aside.

7. Use the pattern of the noshi that was left intact, and cut one layer of the iron-on interfacing with the adhesive treatment facing up.

8. Place the pattern of the noshi that was left intact under the interfacing. Trace the lines of the ribbons and the numbers with a very light pencil or chalk. You don't want the pencil showing through the fabric.

Place ribbons close together.

9. Place the interfacing on an ironing board. Take the corresponding ribbons, and place them on the interfacing. When placing the ribbons next to each other, try not to leave any space between them. If there is space, make sure your satin stitches will be wide enough

to cover the space as well as catch enough fabric.

10. When all the ribbon pieces are in place, check to make sure the band fits.

11. Place the rayon chords in the center, where the band is to be placed. Pull two of the outside chords towards the back 1", and pull the middle chord toward the front 1". This will produce chords of varying lengths for the front and back. Replace the band.

12. Cover the noshi with a pressing cloth and press. When the pieces are somewhat anchored, turn the noshi over, cover with a pressing cloth, and press.

13. Set your sewing machine to a wide satin stitch and the appropriate stitch length. Use your appliqué, open-toe foot, which will allow you to see the stitches.

14. Thread your machine with black rayon thread in the top. Use black sewing thread in your bobbin. Test your satin stitch with straight and curved lines of stitching. Check to see if the bobbin thread is coming up above your fabric. If it is, adjust your tension. Loosen the top tension by small increments until the stitch is perfect.

15. Place the noshi on a lightweight tear-away stabilizer and pin in several places.

16. Start all your lines of

satin stitching at the edge of the band. (Later all these starting points will be covered up by the stitching around the band.)

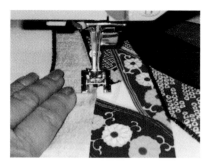

The satin stitch must cover any spaces and catch fabric from both sides.

17. Look at all the ribbon pieces. Notice that some ribbon pieces are on top and some are coming from underneath. Sew the sides of the ribbons that are underneath. When you sew the ones that are on top, you will be covering the starting points of the previous ribbons.

18. Sew a preliminary satin stitch around the perimeter. (Later, to attach the noshi to the jacket, use the same wide width of satin stitch already used on the ribbons.)

19. Tear away the stabilizer. If the stabilizer does not fall away easily, place your finger on the stitching, and press down while tearing the stabilizer away horizontally with the other hand. Set the noshi aside, because it cannot be applied to the jacket until the shoulder seam is sewn.

Large waves

The large wave on the back of the jacket is cut from a light tan dupioni silk and embellished with teal rayon thread and teal variegated rayon thread. The variegated rayon thread has a beautiful gradation of color and offers a nuance of difference, while sharing the same color.

1. Trace the motif onto the tan silk and place a layer of Soft 'n Sheer and lightweight stabilizer underneath. Pin in several places.

Start with the small curling waves, using the variegated rayon threads. Then sew the larger waves with teal rayon thread.

2. Thread your machine with the variegated teal thread. Set your machine with a narrow width satin stitch, and start with the small curling waves.

3. With each set, start with the curling wave on top. Start at the beginning of the curl, and use a few stitches in reverse to anchor. Sew the curl, ending at the crest of the next wave.

4. Once again, start at the beginning of the curl and follow the curve to the next crest, if there is one. (Each curling wave below covers up the ending of the wave above.)

5. When all the curls are completed, sew a narrow preliminary satin stitch around the perimeter of the entire motif.

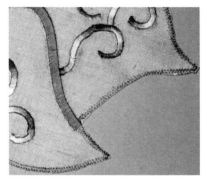

Sew a preliminary satin stitch around the perimeter. Cut close to the edge.

6. Remove the tear-away stabilizer. Cut the tan dupioni and Soft 'n Sheer close to the preliminary stitching edge.

7. Lightly coat the back of the large wave with spray adhesive, and place it on the appropriate place on the back of the jacket. Smooth and press in place with your fingers.

8. Cut two layers of lightweight tear-away (used together to create a medium weight) larger than the motif, and place them underneath the jacket fabric. Pin in several places.

9. Thread your machine with the teal rayon thread. Sew a preliminary straight stitch around the perimeter of the large wave to keep it in place.

10. Satin stitch the bottom of the wave with a medium width. Start sewing the wave lines from right to left. (Each wave to the left will cover the ending stitches of the previous wave to the right.)

11. Start each line with a "0" width, quickly adjusting to a wider width while in motion. Do a test on scrap fabric to get accustomed to tapering and achieving a consistent appearance.

Use wide satin stitching for the tops of the waves.

Small waves

The small waves on the front of the gold jacket are just a portion of the large waves. The small wave is traced right onto the jacket fabric. The same threads are used. The same satin stitch technique is used. There is no preliminary perimeter stitching.

1. Cut two layers of lightweight tear-away larger than the small wave motif, and place them underneath the jacket fabric. Pin in several places.

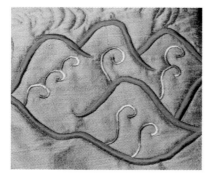

Use a wide satin stitch in the final sewing around the perimeter.

2. Start with the small curling waves, using the variegated rayon thread. Start the perimeter waves from the right, following the same procedure that you used to make the large waves.

Pagoda

The pagoda is cut from the same dark purple dupioni silk used as one of the ribbons for the noshi. It is then outlined with bright orange satin stitching, which is another color found in the ribbons of the noshi.

1. The pagoda lines are traced onto purple dupioni silk.

2. The pagoda is a small motif, so the shape is cut out,

and the back is lightly coated with spray adhesive. Place the pagoda on the appropriate area of the jacket fabric. Smooth and press with your fingers.

3. Cut a layer of lightweight tear-away larger than the motif, and place it underneath the jacket fabric. Pin in several places.

4. Thread your machine with orange rayon thread, and set it to a straight stitch. Sew over all the lines and the perimeter to anchor the pagoda.

5. Set your machine to a medium satin stitch width. Satin stitch over the straight stitch guidelines. Start the satin stitching with the short vertical lines across the center of the pagoda. Cover the beginning and ending stitches with the stitching of the roof and then the supporting legs.

Cherry blossoms

The cherry blossoms are made in two sizes. There are

four small and two large flowers. Six different fabrics are used. Some of the same fabrics and colors from the noshi are used to create a similarity, without being exactly the same. The same black rayon thread is used but with a narrow to medium satin stitch width.

1. Trace the lines of the cherry blossom onto the fabrics you have selected. Cut them out, and lightly coat the backs with spray adhesive. Place them on the right front side of the jacket. Overlap some of them. Smooth and press with your fingers.

2. Cut a layer of lightweight tear-away stabilizer larger than the motif, and place it underneath the jacket fabric. Pin in several places.

3. Thread your machine with the black rayon thread, and sew a preliminary straight stitch around the edges of all the flowers.

4. Set your machine to a narrow to medium width satin titch, and cover the edge of the fabric and preliminary straight stitch. Satin stitch around the flowers that are partially covered by another flower.

5. Then satin stitch around the flowers that are on top, covering the beginnings and endings of the flowers beneath.

6. Add a few beads in the center of the flowers. Use a few bugle beads for shine or round beads for texture.

For the black jacket

Crane

The crane is created from white fabric, which can be something as lightweight as dupioni silk or as heavy as obi fabric. A lustrous fabric will look great with the silky rayon and shiny metallic gold thread.

1. Using erasable ink or a light touch with a pencil, trace the crane onto white fabric. Don't trace the gold free-motion lines inside the feathers.

2. If your white fabric is lightweight, line it with another layer of white fabric or Soft 'n Sheer after tracing the lines.

3. Cut two layers of lightweight tear-away stabilizer larger than the motif, and place them underneath the white fabric. Pin the stabilizer in several places.

4. Do not cut the fabric close to the crane. (There is a lot of stitching, and you may want to use a hoop.)

5. Thread your machine with a white rayon thread. Use a narrow width satin stitch for the lines on the crane. Look carefully at the feathers. If you start the feathers at the bottom of the wings, each layer of feathers

above it will cover the beginnings and endings of the feathers below. The feathers on the crane are small and close together. Remember to pivot during those tight curves.

6. Use gold metallic thread to shade inside the feathers.

7. After all the stitching inside the crane is completed, the perimeter will need a preliminary satin stitch. Then remove the tear-away stabilizer.

Free-motion with gold metallic threads to create details inside the feathers.

The lines of feathers on the white crane have been covered with satin stitching. The red crown on its head has been sewn, and the crane is placed on the back of the jacket.

8. The outline of the crane will be cut and applied to the jacket fabric. Place tear-away stabilizer under the jacket fabric. Use a medium satin stitch to outline the body.

9. The crown of the crane's head is stitched with red rayon thread. Use a narrow width of satin stitch to sew the curve of the top and the curve of the bottom. As you approach the area near the beak, the crown tapers to meet the beak. Reduce the width of the satin stitch to taper to a point. Fill in the center area with more satin stitching.

10. The throat area is black. Use black rayon or black metallic thread. The part of the throat area that meets the beak is tapered. Use the same tapering technique as used with the crown.

11. Two narrow lines of gold satin stitching are sewn on both sides of the black throat area. The gold beak is added, covering the white fabric. It too requires the tapering technique.

12. Add a bead for the eye.

13. Use the same black for the tail feathers as used for the throat. Fill in the tail feathers using narrow to medium width satin stitching, and outline the feathers in gold.

Pine trees

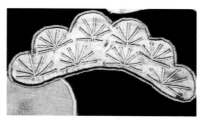

The pine trees are traced onto a light silvery green dupioni silk and placed on the back right side of the black jacket. Two sizes of boughs are used. The little bursts of lines inside the pine tree shapes represent the pine needles. The brown curved shapes underneath represent the branches.

1. Trace and cut out one large and two small pine tree shapes, and lightly coat the backs with adhesive spray.

2. One large and one small pine tree are placed above the

serene waters on the jacket fabric. Smooth and press the motif in place with your fingers.

3. Cut a layer of lightweight tear-away stabilizer larger than the motifs, and place it underneath the jacket fabric. Pin in a few places.

4. Thread your machine with a silvery gray rayon thread for the pine needles, and later use avocado green for the perimeter of the pine trees. Backstitch to anchor the needles.

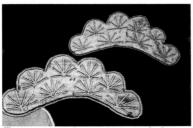

The pine tree at the top is satin stitched using a narrow width. The pine tree at the bottom is satin stitched with a medium width. The small dark spot at the lower right corner of the large pine tree is a mark made from excess Fray Check.

5. Use a very narrow width for the pine needles, and then use a width slightly wider than the pine needles to satin stitch the perimeter of the smaller pine tree.

6. Use slightly wider widths for the larger pine tree.

7. Use the same methods of preparation for the small pine tree in the foreground. Set your machine to a width slightly narrower than medium, and satin stitch the pine needles in avocado green.

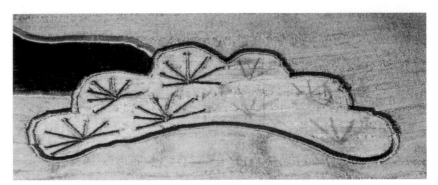

This pine tree is placed close to the bottom of the jacket. To emphasize its position in the foreground, the pine needles are satin stitched in avocado green (a darker color than used on the other pine trees), and the pine tree is sewn around the perimeter with a wider satin stitch.

Remember to backstitch to anchor the tips of the needles.

8. Use a width slightly wider than medium to satin stitch the perimeter of the pine tree in the same avocado green.

9. Draw the curved branches under the pine tree. Thread your machine with a brown rayon thread. Set your machine to a medium to wide satin stitch, and follow the lines.

Fan with ribbon ends

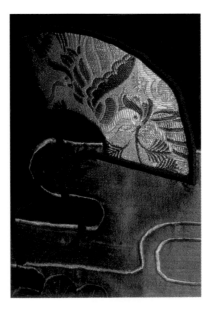

This fan motif is made from the same fan shape as used for the motifs on the right sleeve of the gold jacket. The attached ribbons are created with rayon thread.

1. Cut the fan from a special vintage fabric with colors used somewhere nearby in another motif.

2. Spray the back of the fabric with a light coating of the adhesive spray.

3. Place the fan on the fabric. Smooth and press with your fingers.

4. Cut a layer of lightweight tear-away stabilizer larger than the motif, and place it underneath the jacket fabric. Pin in a few places.

Use the same fan design with a special vintage fabric.

5. Thread your machine with purple rayon thread, and set it to a straight stitch. Sew a preliminary straight stitch around the perimeter of the fan.

6. Set your machine to a wide satin stitch. Satin stitch the bottom curve of the fan and then the top curve of the fan.

7. Place your needle at the left top edge of the fan, and satin stitch the left side of the fan to meet the left bottom edge of the fan. Continue in a straight line for another inch, and then turn your fabric and meander slowly, creating a curved ribbon of thread. Taper the end to a point by narrowing the satin stitch to "0" as you sew. Apply the same procedure for the right side of the fan.

Serene water

The serene water is created to give the background a color that will enhance the motifs placed on it.

1. Trace the lines of the serene water onto gold dupioni silk. Cut out the shape of the serene water, and spray the back of the fabric with a light coating of adhesive spray. Place the motif on the jacket fabric. Smooth and press with your fingers.

2. Cut a layer of lightweight tear-away stabilizer larger than the motif, and place underneath the jacket fabric.

3. Thread the machine with gold rayon thread.

4. Set the machine to a straight stitch, and sew a preliminary stitch around the perimeter. Create a few horizontal lines inside the serene waters. Add curves to have them meander. Use a straight stitch to create guidelines for the satin stitching.

5. To begin satin stitching, set the machine to a medium width satin stitch, and follow the guidelines inside the perimeter. Then satin stitch around the perimeter.

Leaves

The leaves for the peonies are created with faux shibori vintage fabric. Shibori is created using a tie-dye method, creating texture and design. In this case, it's cleverly printed and a special weave is used to add texture.

1. Trace the shapes of the leaves and the leaf veins onto the fabric.

2. Cut out the leaf motif, and spray the back with a light coat of spray adhesive.

3. Place the leaves on the serene water. Check to see where you will be placing the peonies to make sure the leaf stems get tucked under the flowers.

4. Cut a layer of lightweight tear-away stabilizer larger than the motif, and place it underneath the jacket fabric. Pin in a few places.

5. Thread the machine with the same avocado green thread used for the pine trees. Sew a preliminary straight stitch around the leaves and cover the preliminary stitches with a medium to wide satin stitch. (Optional: Cover the stitches with a wide satin stitch. The wide satin stitch and the raised thickness will emphasize the motifs in the foreground.)

6. Start with the leaf veins. For the half leaves, start the veins at the leaf centers, and sew toward the leaf edges.

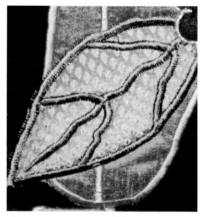

Create realistic veins on the leaves.

Wiggle the fabric as you satin stitch to create curved lines as found in nature. Taper the ends of the veins.

7. For the full leaves, start at the base of the stem and sew down the center of the leaf, wiggling it to match the other veins. When you approach the tip of the leaf, start to taper the center vein. Add veins, starting at the center vein and sewing towards the leaf edges.

8. For the perimeter of the leaves, use the same medium to wide satin stitch. Start at the base of the stem, sewing down one side of the leaf, turning at the point, and sewing back up the other side of the leaf. Then cover with a wide satin stitch.

Peonies

The peonies are created separately and then placed on the jacket. Two sizes of the flower are used. Lavender, gold, and orange rayon threads are used on both flowers. Purple rayon thread is used on the fuchsia dupioni, and fuchsia rayon thread is used on the purple dupioni.

1. Cut a square piece of purple dupioni, Thermore, Soft 'n Sheer stabilizer, and lightweight tear-away stabilizer larger than the motif. Place them in that order with the purple dupioni on top. Pin in a few places.

Layers made up of dupioni silk, Thermor, Soft 'n Sheer, and lightweight tear-away stabilizer. The peony is traced with a chalk pencil.

2. Trace the petal lines of the peony onto the purple dupioni. Thread your machine with orange thread and set to a straight stitch. Sew over the lines.

The chalk lines are covered with a straight stitch, using orange rayon thread.

3. Set your machine for a narrow satin stitch, and cover

the lines inside the peony, but don't satin stitch the perimeter lines.

Use a narrow satin stitch over the preliminary orange straight stitch.

4. Thread your machine with fuchsia rayon thread, and set your machine for free-motion.

5. Create striated shading lines inside each petal.

Shade inside the petals, using free-motion and fuchsia rayon thread.

6. Thread the machine with lavender rayon thread. Create striated shading lines inside each petal, in between the fuchsia lines.

Shade between the fuchsia lines with lavender rayon thread.

7. Follow the same procedure for the fuchsia peony. Substitute the fuchsia rayon thread for purple rayon thread.

8. Remove the lightweight tear-away. Cut very closely along the straight stitch edge.

9. If there is any fraying, trim the threads.

10. Spray the back of the peonies with a light coat of adhesive spray, and place the peonies over the serene water and leaves. (Make sure the leaves have been sewn in place first.)

11. Place a layer of lightweight tear-away stabilizer underneath the jacket fabric. Pin in a few places.

12. Thread the machine with a metallic gold, and set to a slightly wider than narrow satin stitch. Stitch the perimeter of the peonies, covering the edges and straight stitch.

Preliminary assembly

1. Separate the two front pieces of dupioni silk, and place them with the right sides facing up.

2. Separate the front pieces that are cut out of batting, and lightly coat them with spray adhesive. Place the dupioni silk front pieces over the batting front pieces.

3. Spray the back of the batting, and place it on the muslin or Soft 'n Sheer.

Preliminary assembly of the dupioni silk, batting, and muslin.

4. Smooth and press with your fingers. Pin in a few places through all of the layers. Place the two front pieces to the side.

5. Sew the center back seam of the dupioni silk back pieces with right sides together. Sew the center back seam of the muslin. Press the seams open. If you are using Soft 'n Sheer in place of the muslin, the sheets are placed side by side without sewing them together. The center back seam allowance for the batting can be cut away and the edges can be placed together.

6. Spray the wrong side of the muslin, and place the batting over it. Spray the batting and place the dupioni silk back over it, with the right side facing up.

7. Smooth and press with your fingers. Pin in a few places through all layers, and set aside.

Making the bias strips

If using a rotary cutter for the first time, please be sure to observe a demonstration of the proper handling and positioning. Work slowly and carefully, keeping your hands away from the path of the rotary cutter.

1. Use your rotary cutter, mat, and ruler to create bias binding. Your mat will show a 45° angle to use in cutting fabric on the bias. Line up your fabric with the horizontal edge at the bottom of the mat, and find the correct angle/line.

2. Line up your rotary cutter with the line and cut. (The 2" width for the bias strip is determined by the fact that my pattern calls for a 1/2" seam allowance. It takes four times the seam allowance to bind the edge. If you are creating a wider or narrower seam binding, your bias strips will be a different width.)

3. From that edge, use your ruler to find the 2" increment, and cut bias strips. A 1/2-yard of fabric is a generous amount to cut approximately 14 feet of bias strips. (You may need more or less depending on the pattern and size used.) Please use long strips to avoid frequent joining of strips.

4. To join the strips, place them with right sides together at a 90° angle.

Join strips and sew.

Press seams open and trim.

Bias strip.

5. Sew from inside corner to inside corner.

6. Press open and trim points.

7. Press in half with wrong sides together. Set aside.

Assembling the jacket

1. All the motifs, except the noshi, have been placed on the fronts and back of the jacket pieces. The noshi cannot be applied until that shoulder seam has been sewn. Carefully, press all the pieces, using a pressing cloth. Use the original pattern to re-cut (and re-shape) each front and the back.

2. Place the left front on the left side of the back with right sides together. Pin along the shoulder/sleeve seam.

3. Sew with the specified seam allowance. Trim away the extra batting and muslin/Soft 'n Sheer. Press the seams open. If your jacket fabric tends to fray, serge the edges or use pinking shears to finish the edges.

4. Lay the jacket flat with the right side up, so you can apply the noshi to the left shoulder. Place the band at the shoulder seam if possible. Adjust the noshi until you are pleased with the placement.

5. Lay the noshi flat on the jacket shoulder, and pin around the perimeter and in several places in the center. Using a wide width of satin stitch, sew around the perimeter of the noshi with black rayon thread.

Satin stitch around the perimeter.

6. Place the right front on the right back with right sides together. Sew the shoulder/sleeve seam. Trim the excess batting and muslin from the seam allowance, and finish the fabric edge if needed.

7. Place the sleeve/side seams with right sides together. Pin. Sew the seams. Trim the excess batting and muslin from the seam allowances, and finish the fabric edges if needed. Clip the curve under the arm.

8. Place the lining front on the lining back with right sides together. Sew the shoulder/sleeve and the sleeve/side seams. Trim seams, and clip the curve under the arms.

9. Place the lining sleeves inside the jacket sleeves with wrong sides together. Pin around the perimeter of the jacket. The lining may appear larger than the jacket. Try the jacket on, and see if the lining still shows. If it does, trim and pin again.

10. Check to see if the sleeves are the correct length. (Remember, you may need shoulder pads.) Trim the sleeve length if it's too long.

11. Apply the bias seam binding. The very beginning of the bias strip is the raw edge of fabric. Turn the edge back 1/2" toward the wrong side. Place this folded edge at the bottom edge of the side seam. Place the bias strip on the jacket edge with right sides together. Loosely place the bias strip around the perimeter and pin. Be extra careful with the curves, and allow ease to avoid puckering.

12. When you get back to the side seam where you began, overlap the beginning for a 1/2" and cut the bias strip.

13. Sew around the perimeter of the bias with a 1/2" seam allowance. Turn the bias strip over the seam allowance, and tuck the edges under on the other side.

14. On the other side, place the tucked edge over the thread of the previous seam. Pin. Hand sew in place.

Adding Embellishment

Refer to the section on Adding embellishment (page 43) for techniques, and use your creativity to add extra flair to your jacket.

1. Add beads to the centers of the flowers.

2. Create tassels with beads, and add them to a decorative pin to use as a closure for the front of your jacket.

3. Use a bead for the eye of the crane.

Heart of a Golden Dragon

This ensemble was designed for the Fairfield Fashion Show 2000-2001. It was a significant year. It was the Year of the Golden Dragon, a dragon of the Five Sacred Elements and celebrated only once every sixty years. What a great year to be a part of the show.

Supplies

❈ Pattern: modified Nouveau Kimono© by Kimura
❈ Purple dupioni silk for the entire jacket
❈ Dupioni silk: Turquoise, teal, light green, dark green, fuchsia, and lavender
❈ Purple chiffon

❈ Fairfield's Poly-fil® Low-Loft® batting
❈ TWE/Beads: Bugle beads, Swarovski crystals, rhinestones
❈ Beading needles
❈ Pre-waxed twisted nylon thread
❈ Monofilament thread

❈ Decorative threads: Sliver Metallics, rayon, and metallic in a variety of colors
❈ Spray adhesive
❈ Stabilizers
❈ Lightweight iron-on interfacing
❈ Asian fabric sources: Zenga and Texuba

The ensemble includes a rich, royal purple dupioni silk kimono. This kimono is a fusion of traditional and contemporary style. The sleeves are modern, richly embroidered with lightning bolts of gold metallic, and dripping with tassels of silk threads and pearls. The traditional collar is encrusted with faceted rhinestones. On the back of the kimono is a golden dragon ablaze with bugle beads and Swarovski crystals, riding a flashing thundercloud.

Spools and spools of Sliver Metallic thread and many strands of bugle beads are used for the motifs on this garment. Purple lightning streams down from the shoulders, covering the entire top portion of the kimono, while gold bolts of lightning flash upward from the gold cuffs.

The back of the kimono is ablaze with the fiery dragon with its features outlined in ridges of thick black rayon thread and filled in with beads. He sits on highly embroidered clouds of sparkling metallic threads. The clouds are lined in silver, of course, and gold lightning bolts streak down from the clouds, echoed with purple rayon thread.

Meanwhile, the front of the kimono is a calm scene of lotus flowers and leaves, shaded with jewel-tone rayon and metallic threads. Elegant irises are framed by wide bands of Sliver Metallic thread in fan shapes. The lower front

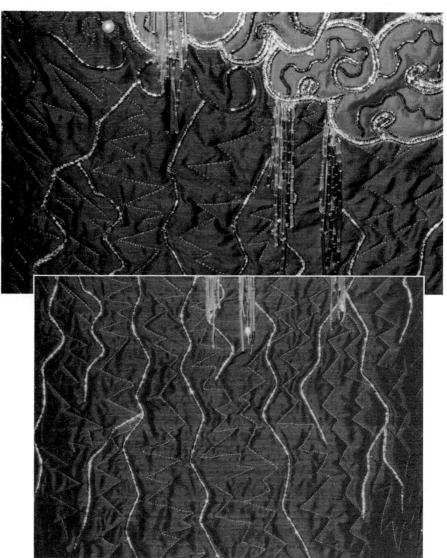

Lightning bolts of satin stitching are echoed by angular free-motion.

half of the kimono is quilted with sheer opalescent Sliver Metallic threads.

Under the kimono is a skirt of layers of flowing chiffon with a hem edged in silky rayon threads. The heart-shaped neckline frames the diamond necklace that holds a golden heart.

The stylized obi belt is shaped and embellished to flatter. The traditional obi cord is draped to the side and embellished with beaded tassels.

Patterns

The Nouveau Kimono pattern is modified by adding pleats to the shoulders, creating a fuller kimono with a more dramatic effect. The front hem is tapered down to the back and resembles a cocoon shape to show off more of the chiffon skirt. An extra collar of brocade peeks out from behind the gold collar, and gold piped cuffs are added for balance.

The skirt pattern is just a complete circle. The halter top and obi belt patterns are included with the pattern for the Nouveau Kimono.

The skirt and halter

The halter top is basically a soft, wide cummerbund with gathered chiffon for the bust area. The straps taper and tie in the back of the neck. You can use this style of pattern or any kind of top that suits you.

The elegant, flowing chiffon skirt is a perfect contrast for the quilted, shaped kimono. The directions to create this skirt are offered, but feel free to substitute a skirt of your choice or even slacks.

1. The skirt is cut from layers of chiffon and a matching lining. The shape of the pattern is a complete circle. For a floor length skirt, you'll need the measurement from your waist to the desired hem length, plus a few inches.

2. Measure your hips. Use

that measurement for the circumference of the inner circle.

3. From the inner circle, use your tape measure to mark a concentric circle an even distance away from the inner circle. Use the measurement taken from Step 1 for the distance from your waist to the desired hem length, plus a few inches.

4. Cut the pattern in half, creating two semi circles, and

place the side seams on the selvage. You will need two halves for each layer. Use as many layers as you like.

5. Place the semi circles on a single layer of fabric to accommodate the length of the skirt.

6. Do the same for the lining.

7. Sew the selvage side seams for each pair of semi circles. Press the seams open.

8. Layer all the circles, with the lining as the bottom layer.

9. Cut a waistband casing, and attach it to the circumference of the inner circle.

10. Thread with elastic to fit your waist, while allowing it to slide over your hips.

11. Let the un-hemmed skirt hang for a day or two. The parts of the skirt that are on the bias will stretch to their maximum length.

12. Trim the hem evenly.

13. Finish the hem with rayon thread on the serger, using the rolled hem technique.

14. Go over the hem with a second layer of rayon thread for a well defined, rolled hem.

The obi belt

The traditional obi is thick and wide. It wraps and wraps around the waist. I did just the opposite when creating this obi. An exaggerated, curved, pieced pattern is designed to create a shapely peplum effect. Sliver Metallic thread is used to embellish the front of the obi with a chrysanthemum. The thread is perfect in mimicking the vintage Asian brocade used for the obi.

The obi cord indicates a woman's age by its placement horizontally on the obi. A younger woman places the cord higher up on the obi. As a symbolic gesture of agelessness, the cords on this contemporary obi are tied and draped to the side. The tassels at the end of the cords are beaded with lustrous pearls. The Obi belt pattern is included with the Nouveau Kimono pattern. Or you can embellish your own creation.

The kimono

The Nouveau Kimono pattern is modified to look contemporary with just an allusion to the traditional kimono. Gathered pleats are added to the shoulders to create drama and accommodate larger motifs. The shape of the hem is altered to show off more of the chiffon skirt.

The sleeves are still quite full and pleated at the wrist. Cuffs piped in gold are added to match the collar. Embellished tassels are added to the cuffs to draw your eyes there.

The traditional collar is layered with a wider second collar. Both are extended down the front of the kimono and end with more tassels. The gold top layer of the collar is beaded with several sizes of rhinestones, crystal sequins, and beads.

Fabric

Dupioni silk is used for the entire kimono because of its lustrous, shimmering threads. A deep purple makes up the entire kimono, with gold accenting the cuffs and collar. The motifs are embellished using dupioni silks in jewel tones. The clouds on the back are made of a lighter weight dupioni in teal and turquoise. The body of the dragon is made of vintage obi, using the reverse side of the metallic fabric. The extra layer of collar and the obi are created with turquoise and gold vintage brocade.

Motifs

Select a few or use all of the motifs (the templates are in chapter 5). Reduce and enlarge them to fit the pattern in your size. When the motifs are the right size, arrange them on the modified kimono pattern. Check to make sure everything fits and that the proportions are pleasing. Then, transfer the designs to the fabrics.

The motifs created with just thread—fans, serene water, lightning bolts, and curling mist—are traced onto the fabric before adding batting, and stabilizers. The outlines of the other motifs are set aside for placement later.

The fans on the right front are created using blue, fuchsia, and green threads with the satin-stitch technique. The machine is set to a medium width and two lines of satin stitching are sewn side by side to outline the fans. The designs inside the fans are created using free-motion and satin stitching.

The serene waters are created with satin stitching in straight and curved lines, using a medium to wide satin stitch and turquoise thread.

Lightning

1. The lightning bolts (elongated jagged lines of motion in varying lengths) are drawn with a chalk pencil onto the fronts, back, and sleeves of the purple dupioni silk kimono pieces. Some of the zig-zags branch off to create smaller zigzags. These lightning bolts are used to fill the spaces and aid in artfully keeping the batting in place.

2. First, use a medium width satin stitch and move the fabric to the left and right to create the jagged lines. The lightning bolts are then sewn a second time with a medium to wide satin stitch. This creates a raised and dramatic line, since the threads are the same color as the fabric and the effect could be too subtle. When ending a lightning bolt, taper it to a "0" width, and then stitch in place for a few stitches to anchor the threads.

3. The same technique as above is used for the gold lightning bolts.

Curling mist

1. Turquoise Sliver Metallic thread is used to create the curling mist on the sides of the clouds. The mist is satin stitched in a medium width and then stitched over again with a medium to wide stitch.

2. Smooth curls are created by slowly turning the fabric while sewing.

Lotus flower

The lotus flowers are highly embellished with free-motion stitching. A few petals are not embellished. This differentiates them as the backs of the petals. The rest of the petals are shaded using two colors.

The insides of the petals are filled with the same color as the backs of the petals, but in a different shade. The tips are shaded with a color that creates contrast.

Opalescent and rose threads are used for the lavender flower, and rose and dark purple threads are used for the fuchsia flower. The flowers are satin stitched around the perimeter with gold thread in a narrow to medium width.

The lotus flowers and leaves are created separately and then placed on the jacket. Two flowers are made in the same size and four leaves are made in two different sizes.

1. Cut a large enough square piece of fuchsia dupioni silk, and trace the lotus flower motif. Also cut Thermore, Soft 'n Sheer, and lightweight tear-away stabilizer, and place in that order behind the fuchsia dupioni silk. Pin in a few places, through all the layers.

2. Thread your machine with gold metallic thread. Follow the petal lines using a preliminary straight stitch or free-motion.

3. Set your machine to a narrow to medium satin stitch. Sew over the preliminary straight stitch, still using the gold metallic thread.

4. Change the thread to a dark purple Sliver Metallic thread. Use free-motion to shade the inside of the tips of the petals. Use a back and forth motion to create striated shading lines in varying lengths. Check the photograph to see the shading used on the tips of the petals.

5. Change the thread to a light purple Sliver Metallic thread. Use free-motion to shade the inside bottom portion of the petals. Use longer, striated shading lines and vary the lengths. Make the shading denser where it is closer to the center of the flower. The shading is less dense as it moves up the petal.

6. Cut around the perimeter of the flower, close to the satin stitching. Sew beads or sequins in the center of the flower. Set aside.

7. Cut a large enough square piece of lavender dupioni silk, and trace the lotus flower motif. Also cut Thermore, Soft 'n Sheer, and lightweight tear-away stabilizer. Place them in that order behind the light purple dupioni silk. Pin in a few places and through all the layers.

8. For the fuchsia lotus flower, use the same methods as used for the lavender lotus flower. Start with the gold metallic thread around the petals. In place of the dark purple Sliver Metallic thread used on the tips on the inside of the petals, use the rose Sliver Metallic thread. In place of the light purple Sliver Metallic thread used to shade the bottom of the petals, use the opalescent Sliver Metallic thread.

9. Cut around the perimeter of the flower, close to the satin stitching. Sew beads or sequins in the center of the flower. Set aside.

The background of the lotus flower and leaves is quilted with sheer opalescent threads.

Lotus Leaves

The lotus flower leaves are filled in the center with satin stitching of various widths. The widths are changed while the fabric is moved left and right, creating a zigzag motion. The widths and movement are done randomly. Avocado and pastel yellow-green rayon threads are used in the satin stitching, and opalescent thread is used to free-motion and outline the satin stitching.

1. Trace and cut two of the smaller leaves out of the dark green dupioni silk.

2. Trace and cut two of the larger leaves out of the light green dupioni silk.

3. Cut Thermore, Soft 'n Sheer, and lightweight tear-away stabilizer in that order, and place a set behind both colors of leaves.

4. Thread the machine with gold metallic thread, and set to a medium width satin stitch. Sew around the perimeter of all four of the leaves.

5. Change the thread to a 30-weight avocado rayon thread, and start with the light green dupioni silk. Begin the satin stitching from the top center of the leaf. All the lines begin from one central point and radiate out. Start the satin stitching with an almost "0" width. After about a half an inch, start to use a wider stitch. Use your right hand to control the stitch width, turning it wider and narrower as your left hand moves the fabric to the left and to the right. When you get close to the gold metallic thread outlining the leaf, start to taper the line to a point. Stitch in place for a few stitches, anchoring the thread. Do the same for the other light green leaf.

6. Change the thread to a 30-weight pastel yellow-green rayon thread. This thread is used on the dark green dupioni silk. Use the same methods as explained above. Complete both leaves.

7. Change the thread to the opalescent Sliver Metallic thread, and prepare your machine for the free-motion technique. This thread will be used on all the leaves. Use this thread in between the striated, rayon satin stitched lines on the leaves. Echo the zigzagged lines. This thread will enhance any color and add a sparkling effect.

8. Cut around the perimeter of the leaves, close to the satin stitching.

9. Place the flowers and leaves on the jacket, over the serene waters.

10. Thread your machine with the gold metallic thread, and set it to a wider satin stitch than is used around the flowers and leaves. Apply the flowers and leaves to the jacket fabric with the satin stitch.

Irises

The irises are created in two parts. The leaves are embellished with wiggling lines of opalescent, purple, and gold threads. They are placed over the fans, and the stems are satin stitched with gold thread in a wide width. The flower portion is created with hand-dyed silks in shades of periwinkle and magenta. The flowers are shaded using free-motion with dark blue thread. The flower portion is placed over the leaves and anchored with gold metallic satin stitching in a narrow width.

1. Trace and cut three sets of iris leaves and stems out of the dark green silk dupioni. Also cut Thermore, Soft 'n Sheer, and lightweight stabilizer in that order, and place them under the dupioni silk.

2. Thread your machine with gold metallic thread, and set to a narrow width satin stitch. Satin stitch around the perimeter of the irises and over the lines that define the leaves and stems. Then use a medium width satin stitch over the lines that define the stem.

3. Change your thread to the turquoise Sliver Metallic thread, and set to a narrow width satin stitch. Sew wiggly lines up and down the leaves. Move the fabric gently to the left and right to create the softly curved lines. The wiggly lines go in another direction down the bent leaves. Repeat this method for all three leaves.

4. Change to the Sliver Metallic opalescent thread, and prepare your machine for free-motion. Sew wiggly lines, echoing the turquoise satin stitched lines. Fill in the leaves with the opalescent thread lines to add sparkle. Repeat this method for all three leaves.

5. Cut large enough sections of hand-dyed silks, and trace three iris flowers. Cut Thermore, Soft 'n Sheer, and lightweight stabilizer in that order, and place them under the hand-dyed silk.

6. Thread your machine with gold metallic thread, and set to a narrow width satin stitch. Satin stitch over the lines that define the perimeter and details of the iris flower.

7. Prepare your machine for free-motion, keeping the gold metallic thread. Loosely free-motion inside the centers of the iris petals.

8. Change the thread to the opalescent Sliver Metallic and free-motion inside the centers of the iris petals. The mixture of the gold and opalescent threads is a nice contrast to the magenta and periwinkle petals.

9. Change the thread to sapphire blue Sliver Metallic thread. Free-motion with striated lines inside the petals to shade the tips and area close to the center. The shading frames the hand-dyed silk petals.

10. Cut around the perimeter of the iris flowers, close to the satin stitching.

11. Place the leaves and stems over the fans on the front of the kimono. Pin in place.

12. Place the iris flowers at the top of the leaves and stems. Pin in place. Use a wider satin stitch to apply the flowers, leaves, and stems.

Teal clouds

The clouds are cut from turquoise and teal dupioni silk and overlapped slightly. The turquoise clouds are embellished with silver, sapphire blue, and turquoise Sliver Metallic threads and curls of wide satin stitching. Apply the same method for the teal clouds, but with silver, dark purple, and mint green stitching. A gold dragon's claw appears from the clouds, holding a large pearl.

1. Trace and cut the one large cloud and a small cloud out of the turquoise dupioni silk. Also cut Thermore, Soft 'n Sheer, and lightweight stabilizer in that order, and place them under the dupioni silk.

2. Thread the machine with silver Sliver Metallic thread, and use a medium width satin stitch to outline the perimeter of the clouds.

3. Change the thread to sapphire blue, and set the satin stitch to a wide width. Sew inside the perimeter of the clouds, along the Sliver Metallic satin stitching. Backstitch at the end of the curls to lock the threads.

4. Optional: Change the thread to turquoise Sliver Metallic, and change the satin stitch to a slightly narrower width. Meander wiggly lines all over the clouds.

5. Trace the two small clouds, and cut them out of the teal dupioni silk. Also cut Thermore, Soft 'n Sheer, and lightweight stabilizer in that order, and place under the silk.

6. Thread the machine with silver Sliver Metallic thread, and repeat the method used for the larger cloud in Step 2. Change the thread to dark purple Sliver Metallic thread and repeat Step 3. Optional: Change the thread to mint green and repeat Step 4.

Dragon's claws

1. Trace and cut the dragon's claw out of gold metallic obi fabric. Also cut Soft 'n Sheer and two layers of lightweight stabilizer, and place them underneath the gold metallic fabric.

2. Thread the machine with gold Sliver Metallic thread and set to a medium width satin stitch to outline the perimeter of the dragon's claw.

3. Change the thread to black Sliver Metallic thread, and set you machine for free-motion. Fill in the three claws, using a back and forth motion.

4. Sew the large pearl at the bottom of the claws.

Teal clouds with the dragon's claw clutching a pearl.

The golden dragon

1. Trace the entire dragon body onto a lightweight tear-away stabilizer, which will be used as a stencil.

2. The portion of the pattern with the long, thin flames is traced onto the back of the kimono, and the shape of the dragon body is traced for placement later.

3. Tear-away stabilizer is placed under the layers of kimono, (purple silk dupioni, batting, and Soft 'n Sheer) where the long thin flames are to be sewn with satin stitching. Pins and basting stitches are used to keep the area flat and taut.

4. The long, thin flames are stitched with gold Sliver Metallic thread. Three rows of narrow width satin stitching, placed side by side, are used to fill in the width. As the flames curl and meander away, the width is tapered to two rows, and then one row tapered to a point.

5. Each gold flame is outlined with red Sliver Metallic thread. The same medium width is used and again tapered at the tips of the flames.

6. Use dark purple Sliver Metallic thread to create lightning bolts in between the long, thin flames. The same method is used as on the shoulders of the kimono.

7. Trace the lines of the dragon body onto the gold metallic obi fabric. The gold obi fabric is placed over layers of lightweight batting, Soft 'n Sheer, and tear-away stabilizer. Pin or baste through all of the layers.

8. Use a black rayon thread with a narrow to medium width satin stitch to create the facial features and small flames around the face.

9. Fill in the eye area with silver Sliver Metallic thread, using a wide satin stitch. Add crystal beads for the eyes.

10. Use red Sliver Metallic thread for the streams of fire coming from the dragon's nose. Start with a wide satin stitch, and taper to a point. Use the same thread to fill in the tongue area with rows of satin stitching.

11. Use red and orange Sliver Metallic threads interspersed with gold Sliver Metallic thread, all in medium to wide widths, to satin stitch the outline of the flames. Fill in some of the flames with random satin stitching, which will show up in between the beads.

12. Use black rayon thread in a medium width satin stitch to outline the trunk of the dragon.

13. When all the satin stitching is completed, remove the tear-away stabilizer from under the dragon.

14. The thread colors can serve as a guide for the bead placement. Bead the entire face of the dragon with Swarovski crystal sequins. These have a hole in the center and can be applied easily.

The beads are spaced apart, creating a "polka dot" effect when seen up close. At a distance, it is an explosion of color. The beads can be placed about a 1/2" apart. (Refer to the Adding Embellishment section on page 43 for the needle and thread information. In this case, a monofilament, clear thread is used.)

15. Thread the needle and tie a knot at the end of the thread. Use short lengths of thread to avoid tangling. Send the needle up from under the layers of dragon fabric and through the hole in the center of the sequin. Send the needle back down the side of the sequin. Repeat the process, coming up the center of the sequin and down the opposite side of the sequin. If the garment will be displayed most of the time, this would be enough stitching to hold the sequin. If the garment will be worn, add a few more stitches for stability. Move on to the next sequin. Tie a knot underneath, after several sequins.

16. Use the pre-waxed, twisted nylon threads to apply the bugle beads. Use the basic backstitch method to outline and fill in the flames with bugle beads. Do not bead very close to the edge of the dragon's perimeter, since he still needs to be applied to the kimono. Allow enough space around the edge to sew. Later, this area will be covered over with rows of beading. The beads are long and tubular, so

curves do not look smooth up close. From a distance, they will sparkle and look fine.

17. To outline the dragon with the bugle beads, send the needle up through the fabric and then through two bugle beads. Place the beads close together, and send the needle back down through the fabric at the end of the second bead. Come back up with the needle in the center of the two beads, and go through the second bead again. Then proceed on to the next two beads.

18. To fill in the outlines, place the beads in random directions, sewing only one bead at a time. Send the needle up through the fabric and then through one bugle bead. Send the needle back down through the fabric at the end of the bead. Repeat the process, sewing through each bugle bead twice before moving on to the next bead.

19. Add a few Swarovski crystals here and there on the trunk of the dragon.

20. When the beading is complete (except for the edges), add a small amount of Fray Check to the stitching, outlining the dragon. Let it dry completely. Then cut close to the stitching.

21. Spray the back lightly with adhesive, and place the dragon on the kimono. Sew along the perimeter edge, and cover with beading.

Preliminary Assembly

1. The Nouveau Kimono pattern is modified, creating a fuller kimono with pleats at the shoulder. The hem is angled to create a cocoon effect. The sleeves are made wider to create a fuller sleeve for gathering and adding a cuff.

2. Extra fabric is not added around the perimeter, because most of the motifs will be prepared and then applied. The kimono is full and any minor shrinkage due to stitching will not affect its shape.

3. One back, two fronts, and two sleeves will be cut from the purple silk dupioni, lightweight batting, and Soft 'n Sheer. Bias binding will also be cut and applied later.

4. Cut one collar from the gold dupioni. Cut one collar from the turquoise and gold vintage fabric, but modify the fabric to make it one inch wider and longer than the gold collar. Cut one collar of lightweight batting and Soft 'n Sheer for the gold collar and two strips of interfacing. Cut cuffs from the gold fabric and interfacing.

5. Cut one back, two fronts, and two sleeves from the lining fabric. Set aside.

6. Trace any designs that will be sewn directly onto the purple dupioni silk at this time.

Then place the lightweight batting and Soft 'n Sheer under the purple dupioni silk, and treat it as one piece. Place a few pins or baste to keep all the layers together.

7. Satin stitch the purple Sliver Metallic lightning bolts at the shoulders and sleeves; the gold lightning bolts near the sleeve cuffs and back hem; the three fans on the right side of the front; the serene waters on the left side of the front; and the curling mist on the back.

8. Satin stitch the embellished motifs in their appropriate places.

9. Press with a pressing cloth.

Assembling the Kimono

The tassels

1. Purchase two large, gold tassels, and add dangling beads to the fringe.

2. Use small pearls to continue the design concept of the large pearls used on the back. Refer to the Adding Embellishment section on page 43 to create the dangling beads.

The collar

1. The gold collar: place the gold dupioni silk over the lightweight batting and Soft 'n Sheer. Treat this as one piece. Thread the machine with gold rayon thread, and use free-motion to keep all the layers together. Use a design similar to that of a jigsaw puzzle.

2. Fold the collar in half, and press with a pressing cloth. Bead only one side of the collar, since that is all that will show. Add rhinestones, bugle beads, and Swarovski crystals. Add the interfacing and assemble the collar according to the pattern instructions.

3. The turquoise and gold collar: Add the interfacing and assemble the collar, according to the pattern instructions. Tuck the tassels in each end of the collar before finishing. Press with a pressing cloth.

Cuffs

1. Create cuffs of any style. Commercial patterns as well as sewing books offer detailed instructions in many styles. Instead of cuffs, a bias strip band can be used for a simpler look.

2. The sleeve is pleated to fit the size of the cuff. The cuff is sewn on, and beads are added where the cuffs join. Refer to the Adding Embellishment section (page 43) to create these dangling bead tassels.

The body

1. Pin the pleats at the shoulders. Sew the shoulder seams.

2. Sew the sleeves to each side. Press the seams with a pressing cloth.

3. Sew the side, underarm, and sleeve seams. Trim the seams and excess batting.

4. Clip the curves. Press the seams with a pressing cloth. (Remember to remove any tear-away stabilizer before completing the garment.)

5. Repeat the process for the lining fabric.

6. Place the turquoise and gold collar behind the gold dupioni silk collar, and treat this as one piece.

7. Place the collar on the kimono, according to the pattern instructions.

8. Place the lining with the kimono/collar at the neckline and the wrong sides together. Pin together from edge to edge for the length of the collar. Trim and clip the curves.

9. Turn the lining, and place it inside the kimono with the wrong sides together. Clip through the kimono and lining where the collar begins on both sides. Press with a pressing cloth.

10. Try on the kimono. See if the lining hangs below the kimono. If it does, trim some of it off. Do not trim off too much. Some ease is needed in the fit of the lining.

11. Pin the purple dupioni silk and the lining together, along the curved hem.

Bias binding

1. Refer to the Adding bias strips section of the Maiko Celebration Vest on page 70 for information on creating the bias strips.

2. In this case, a wider bias strip is used. Cut strips 3" wide. The finished seam binding will be about 3/4".

3. Measure around the perimeter of the kimono from collar edge to collar edge, and add a few inches to decide how much bias strip binding will be needed. The binding is needed only to finish this raw edge, since the area around the collar was finished when the lining was applied. Cut the strips and sew the ends together to create one long strip.

4. Start and end the strips with a 1/2" edge folded back to create a finished edge.

5. Start the bias strip binding at one end of the collar. Place the binding edge along the edge of the kimono/lining with right sides together, and continue to the other end of the collar. Sew with a 3/4" seam. Turn the binding over, and fold the edge under. Place the folded edge, so it is covering the seam, and hand stitch in place.

Gong Hee Fat Choy!

(Happy New Year!)

Gallery

More Asian Art Flair

Fans and bamboo for the Empress

More Asian-inspired vests

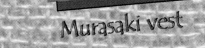
Murasaki vest

Peony magic

Crysanthemum
in bloom

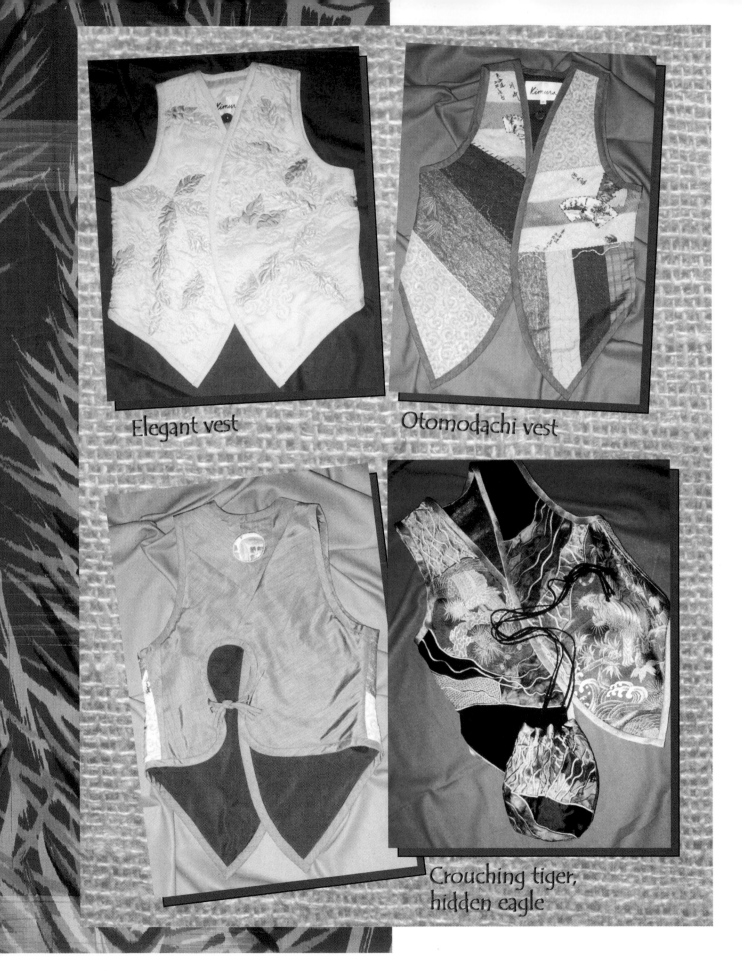

Elegant vest

Otomodachi vest

Crouching tiger,
hidden eagle

Cranes at a festival

Geisha girls wall hanging

The Geisha faces were "tweaked" and grouped together to create a great design. Obi and kimono fabrics were added and dupioni silk created the frame.

Flirting monkey pillow

Chapter 5

Motif Templates

Lotus purse

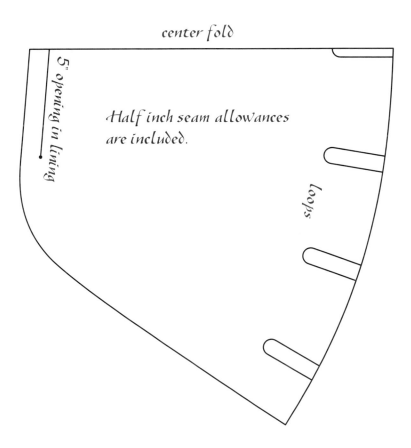

center fold

5" opening in lining

Half inch seam allowances are included.

loops

Photocopy to 200%.

Flowers for the Empress

Leaves

Maiko Celebration

Meandering pine

Chrysanthemum in water

Art to Wear with Asian Flair

Geisha

Tomesode Jacket

Fans

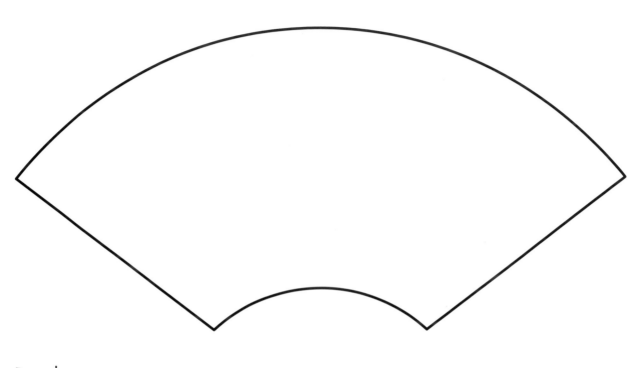

Bamboo

Chrysanthemum

Pagoda

Noshi

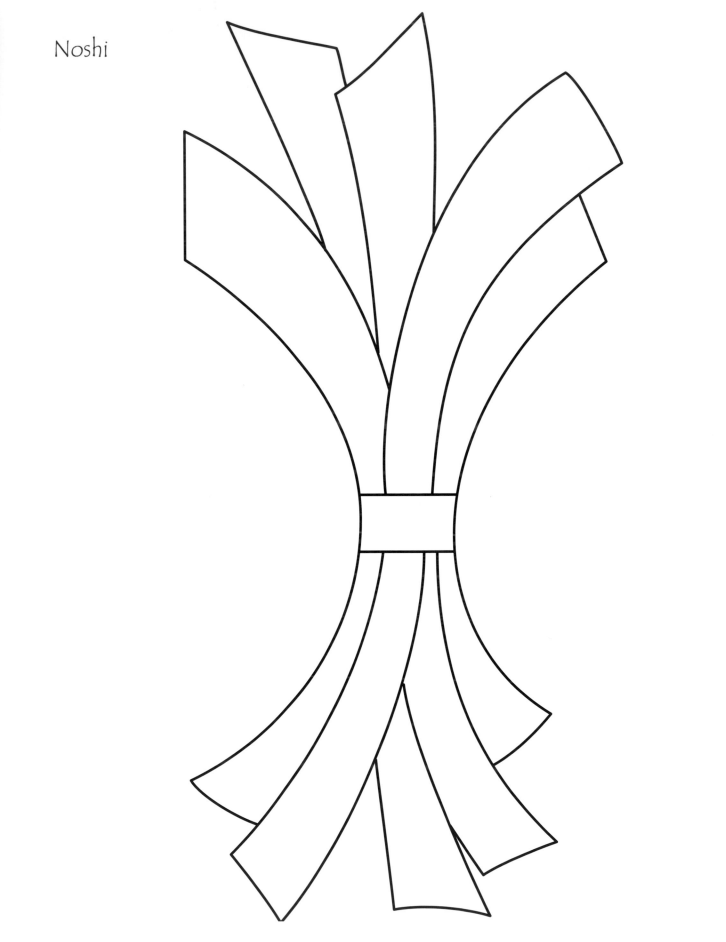

Large waves

Crane

Pine tree

Peonies

Cherry blossoms

Serene waters

Heart of a Golden Dragon

Lotus flower

Lotus leaves

Irises

Dragon's claws

Teal clouds

Golden dragon

More Asian Flair

Flirting monkey

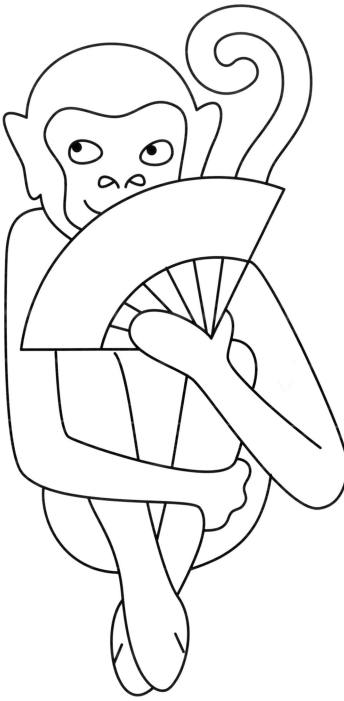

Eyeglass case and practice for decorative stitich

Quarater inch seam allowances are included.

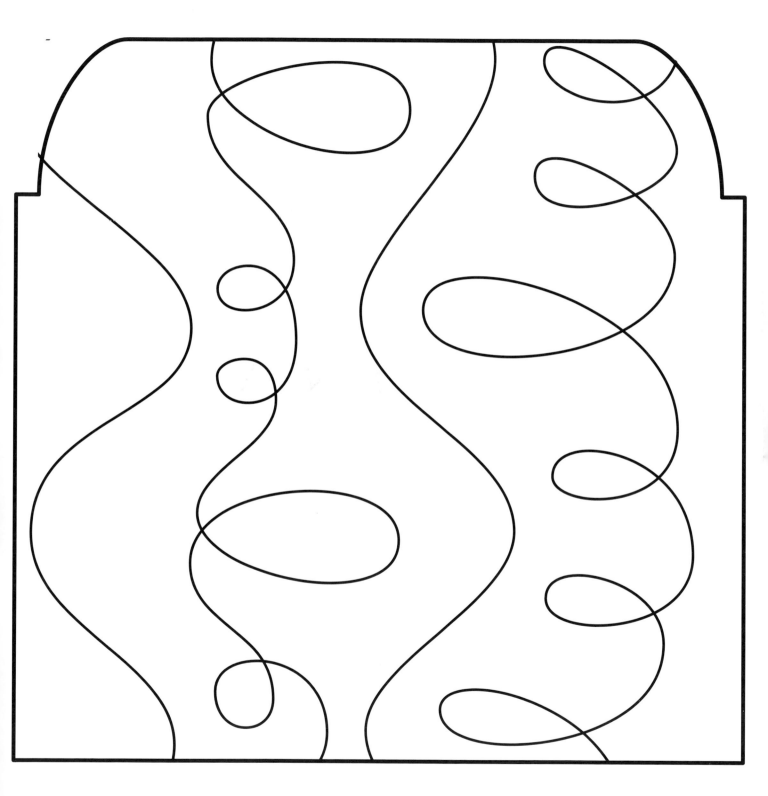

Resources

Asian textiles

Texuba—Marina del Rey, CA—310.827.8535—www.texuba.com

Nichi Bei Bussan—San Jose, CA—408.294.8048—www.nb-store.com

Niu Imports—Laie, HI—808.293.9819

Good Goods—Boyds, MD—301.515.5119—www.good-goods.com

Zenga—Albuquerque, NM—505.275.2209

Quilter's Express to Japan—New York, NY—212.505.0480—www.qejapan.com

Katie's Vintage Kimono—Belfair, WA—360.275.2815—www.katiesvintagekimono.com

Carol Lane Saber Designs—Port Ludlow, WA—360.437.0576—www.saberdesigns.com

Patterns

Pavelka Designs—Gibsons, BC, Canada—www.pavelkadesign.com

Park Bench Patterns—Petaluma, CA—707.781.9142—www.parkbenchpatterns.com

The Sewing Workshop—San Francisco, CA—415.221.SEWS—www.sewingworkshop.com

Diane Ericson—Watsonville, CA—revisions—www.revisions-ericson.com

Ghee's®—Shreveport, LA—318.226.1701—www.ghees.com

June Colburn Designs II—Largo, FL—727.585.8062—www.junecolburn.com

Paw Prints Pattern Co.—Arlington, WA—360.691.4293—www.purrfection.com

Folkwear Patterns—www.larkbooks.com/home.nav/fw/index.html

Kimura patterns

The Quilted Apple—Phoenix, AZ—602.956.0904—www.quiltedapple.com

Eddie's Quilting Bee—Mt.View, CA—888.QUILTER—www.quiltingbee.com

Bearly Stitchin—Pasadena, CA—626.796.2118—www.bearlystitchin.com

Quilted Angel—Petaluma, CA—707.763.0945—www.quiltedangel.com

Fabrics and Finery—San Diego, CA—619.296.3161—www.bazaardelmundo.com

Quilter's Cabin Sewing Centre—Calgary, AB, Canada—403.278.4433—www.quilterscabin.com

Quilt Cabin—Evergreen, CO—303.670.4798

Mare's Bears Quilt Shop—Lewes, DE—302.644.0665—www.maresbearsquiltshop.com

Quilter's Hive—Newark, DE—302.737.5699—www.quiltershive.com

Country Stitches—Coral Springs, FL—954.755.2411—www.countrystitchesonline.com

Rainbow's End—Dunedin, FL—727.733.8572—www.rainbows-end.com

Patches Galore—Ellenton, FL—941.722.5523—come.to/patchesgalore

Once Upon a Quilt—Ft. Lauderdale, FL—www.onceuponaquilt.com

Fabric Mart—Ft. Myers, FL—941.278.5256—www.husqvarnaviking.com

Tomorrow's Heirlooms—Ft. Pierce, FL—561.461.9510

Quilter's Choice—Jupiter, FL—561.747.0525

Queen Ann's Lace—Kissimmee, FL—407.846.7998—www.queenannslace.com

Fabric Warehouse—Lakeland, FL—863.680.1325

Granny's Trunk—Lakeland, FL—863.646.0074

Bob's Sewing Center—Lake Worth, FL—561.965.3077—sewingsl@aol.com

The Quilt Stop—Largo, FL—727.532.4566

Sewing Studio—Maitland, FL—407.831.6488—www.sewing.net

Sunshine Sewing Co. Inc.—Margate, FL—954.971.4810—www.sunshinesewing.com

Great American Quilt Co.—Melbourne, FL—321.984.7505

Quiltscene—Miami, FL—305.969.9886

Suzanne's Quilt Shop—Royal Palm Beach, FL—561.798.0934—www.suzannesquilts.com

Bay Area Sewing—St. Petersburg, FL—727.525.3309

Jay's Fabric Center—St. Petersburg, FL—727.381.6600

Pelican Needlework Shoppe—South Daytona, FL—904.761.8879—www.pelicanquiltworks.com

Mary's Needles & Pins—Stuart, FL—561.220.9198—www.needlesandpins.com

Sew & Sew—Stuart, FL—561.286.8231—www.sewingmachinedealers.com/sewandsew

Bernina Sewing Center—Tampa, FL—888.329.9799—www.berninapfaff.com

Deborah's Quilt Basket—Venice, FL—941.488.6866

Patchwork Station—Macon, GA—912.471.8288—www.mindspring.com/~patchworkstation

Dream Quilters—Tucker, GA—770.939.8034—dreamq@bellsouth.net

Bernina Sewing Center—Honolulu, HI—808.536.6932—berninahi@aol.com

Fabric Mart—Honolulu, HI—808.947.4466—www.fmart.com

Margie's Country Store—Madison, IN—812.265.4429

Seminole Sampler—Catonsville, MD—410.788.1720—www.seminole-sampler.com

Lilies of the Field—Easton, MD—410.822.9117

Needles & Pins—Frederick, MD—301.695.7199—www.needles-n-pins.com

G Street Fabrics—Rockville, MD—301.231.8998—www.gstreetfabrics.com

Jenny's Sewing Studio—Salisbury, MD—410.543.1212—www.jennys-sewing-studio.com

Bears Paw—Towson, MD—800.761.2202—www.bearspaw.com

The Button Box—Needham, MA—877.659.3903—www.buttonboxquiltshop.com

Quilters Point—Mt. Pleasant, MI—517.779.2234—www.quilterspoint.com

Cherrywood Fabrics—Brainerd, MN—888.298.0967—www.cherrywoodfabrics.com

Sewing Bird—Charlotte, NC—704.676.0076—www.sewingbird.com

Ann's Needle & Hook Depot—Franklin, NC—704.524.9626

MACO Crafts—Franklin, NC—828.524.7878

Bernina World of Sewing—Raleigh, NC—919.782.2945—www.sewingmachinedealers.com/berninaworldofsewing

Quilting Possibilities—Bayville, NJ—732.269.8383—www.quiltingposs.com

Crazy Quilters—Highlands, NJ—732.291.7407

A Common Thread—Lake Oswego, OR—503.624.7440—www.acommonthreadfabrics.com

Fabric Mart of Bethlehem—Bethlehem, PA—610.866.3400—www.quilta-holics.com

International Fabric Collection—Erie, PA—814.838.0740—www.intfab.com

Tudor Rose Quilt Shop—Glenmoor, PA—610.458.5255—www.tudor-rose.com

Country Quilt Shop—Montgomeryville, PA—215.855.5554—www.countryquiltshop.com

Souder Store—Souderton, PA—215.723.2017

DYEnamic Fabrics—Columbia, SC—803.695.0307

Quilts by the Bay—Galveston, TX—409.740.9296—www.quiltsbythebay.com

It's a Stitch—Humble, TX—281.446.4999

Fabric Carousel—Huntsville, TX—409.295.8322

Richland Sewing Center—Hurst, TX—817.590.4447

She Did Sew—Katy, TX—281.579.3119—shedidsew@pdq.net

Quilter's Confectionery—Warrenton, VA—540.347.3631—www.quiltsweets.com

Supplies

Bernina of America—Bernina sewing machines—www.bernin-ausa.com

Dharma Trading Co.—Dyes, paints, fabric—800.542.5227—dharmatrading.com

Fairfield—Poly-fil batting—www.poly-fil.com

Rupert, Gibbon & Spider—Dyes, paints, fabric—800.442.0455—jacquardproducts.com

Sulky of America—Threads, stabilizers, adhesives—www.sulky.com

Superior Threads—Threads—800.499.1777—www.superiorthreads.com

Thai Silks—Silk fabric—800.722.7455—www.thaisilks.com

Tsukineko—Inks, stamps, fabric pens—800.796.6633—www.tsukineko.com

TWE Beads—Beads, notions, books—www.twebeads.com

Books

Dalby, Liza Crihfield. *Geisha.* University of California Press, 1983.

Dalby, Liza Crihfield. *Kimono: Fashioning Culture.* Yale University Press, 1993.

Imperatore, Cheryl, and Paul MacLardy. *Kimono Vanishing Tradition: Japanese Textiles of the 20th Century.* Schiffer Publishing, 2001.

Katoh, Amy Sylvester. *Japan: The Art Of Living: A Sourcebook of Japanese Style for the Western Home.* Charles E. Tuttle Co. Inc, 1999.

Tamura, Shuji. *The Techniques of Japanese Embroidery.* Krause Publications, 1999.

Van Riel, Paul. *Kimono.* Hotei Publishing, 2001.

Magazines

Art You Wear published by Rosalie Cooke—408.249.0451—Rosecooke@aol.com

Belle Armoire™ *Art to Wear* published by Stampington & Company—877.STAMPER

Ornament published by Ornament, Inc.—800.888.8950

Sew News published by Primedia—800.289.6397

Somerset Studio™ published by Stampington & Company—877.STAMPER

Threads published by Taunton Press—800.888.8286